HOL

GANG

PAUL SIMONS
&
JOHN CARTER

YELLOW BRICK PUBLISHERS

Copyright @ 1993 by PAUL SIMONS & JOHN CARTER.

The right of PAUL SIMONS & JOHN CARTER to be
identified as the authors of the work has been asserted
by them in accordance with the Copyright, Designs and
Patents Act 1988.

All rights reserved. No part of this publication may be
photocopied, recorded or otherwise reproduced, stored
in a retrieval system or transmitted in any form or by any
electronic or mechanical means without prior permission of the copyright owner and publisher. Any person
who commits any unauthorised act in relation to this
publication may be liable to criminal prosecution and
civil claims for damages.

First Published 1993 by:

YELLOW BRICK PUBLISHERS, 2 LONSDALE ROAD,
QUEENS PARK, LONDON NW6 6RD.

British Library Cataloguing in Publication Data: A catalogue record for this book is available from the British
Library.

ISBN: 0-9520560-6-2

Typeset by: Lonsdale Press.
Printed and bound in Great Britain by:
Cox & Wyman Ltd., Reading, Berkshire.

ACKNOWLEDGEMENTS.

We would like to express our sincerest thanks and appreciation to JOHN KAY. It was often his encouragement that kept the book alive.

We express a special thank-you to YELLOW BRICK PUBLISHERS for their pioneering spirit and commitment to the project.

Especially SAMANTHA BROWNING, whose patience and untiring efforts played a major part in the book's completion.

John & Paul

The Authors and Publishers acknowledge ' THE SUN' newspaper for their kind permission to reproduce articles relating to the Hole-in-One Coup and their untiring campaign to seek justice for the ordinary punter.

They would particularly like to thank The Sporting Life's co-operation in allowing reproduction of numerous articles relating to the 1991 coup; as well as Odds On Magazine, Golf World Magazine, The Daily Star and The Johannesburg Star.

They also wish to acknowledge The Racing Post where the ' At Large ' article was originally published, and would like to express our gratitude to the European P.G.A. for permission to reproduce certain scorecards.

They would also like to express their thanks to Iain Ayre for his editorial advice.

TEED UP FOR A £1,000,000 PAYOUT ▼

Reporting the now fully exposed hole-in-one gambling sting in the September Issue, ODDS ON invited the two smart operators behind it to get in touch . . .

Considering he and his partner probably had close to half a million pounds each tucked away in their bank accounts courtesy of assorted bookies up and down the country, the owner of the voice at the other end of the phone could afford to laugh.

"Do you know what the greatest measure of our coup was?" he asked. "Not just that we made the headlines in the Sun . . . but that our story was so sensational it even knocked the Page Three Girl onto page five!"

It's quite a claim, but then it was quite a coup - arguably the finest gambling sting in the past decade and the man one-half responsible for pulling it off was now revealing to ODDS ON just how it had been done.

"Being keen golf fans, we used to spend our days off watching major tournaments and were surprised at the number of times a yellow disc - denoting a hole-in-one - would appear on the scoreboard; as 'knowledgable' punters we were even more amazed to see that the odds being offered against such an occurrence were far greater than they should have been.

Incredible

And how. The pair started betting on holes-in-one wherever and whenever they could - with incredible results. "We would regularly get 25-1 or 33-1, and often bigger prices than that."

It was an astonishing collective error of judgement by bookmakers; statistically the true odds against a hole-in-one at any major golf tournament are between Evens and 2-1.

"Over three years we won around half a million pounds. But then we found it harder to 'get on' and so this year changed our betting strategy to a series of accumulative bets, which carried even more risk, but in the event proved even more successful."

The men behind the coup are reluctant to reveal their full identities ("just call us John and Paul") - in case their credit accounts are closed - but will admit to having been involved in the bookmaking industry in the past.

Naturally their bets were entirely above board. "We've never colluded with any competitors in any event. And, although for the hole-in-ones we had to plan our strikes on bookmakers throughout the country with military precision, every bet we've ever struck has been legal and above board.

"We merely asked bookmakers to quote us a price about a hole-in-one happening at such-and-such tournament, they would offer a price and we'd accept . . . if we thought it fair. They'd take a position on the outcome and we'd take a contrary one. If they got it wrong, it was because we'd done our homework and they hadn't. It's as simple as that."

Beg to differ

Some small bookmakers have begged to differ, by refusing to pay out. "When we turn up to collect, we've had bookies refusing us payment. All we do is politely enquire on what grounds, request a copy of their rules and refer the matter to the Life's Green Seal Service for arbitration. But most bookmakers accept they've been outwitted and pay up with a smile."

So what next for the deadly duo? "Well, it'll take us a full month to collect all we're owed, then we're off for a good long holiday, when we'll start writing a book on our success."

And then? "And then we'll start planning our next big coup!"

BY DAVID THOMAS

ODDS ON MAGAZINE

ODDS On

"ONE DELUXE FANTASTIC COUP'

This book is based on fact, and the basic details of our hole-in-one coup are as accurate as memory permits, although a little extra flavour may have been added to some of our anecdotes. However, rather than adding insult to injury, the names of some companies and individuals are fictitious unless quoted in press cuttings or existing documentation.

1. THE YELLOW DISC

Summer 1988.

The crowd of golf enthusiasts watching the conveyor belt of changes to the tournament scoreboard gasped in astonishment as the teenage ponytail inserted a Yellow Disk into the sea of colour, signifying of a Hole-in-One.

The murmur of disbelief was as if there had been an unexpected eclipse of the sun, but for my pal John and myself, keen followers of the European Golf tour for more years than we care to remember, this near impossible feat had come as no surprise.

We had been beating the bookies for years with ingenious schemes involving betting on sporting events, and we began to wonder if the bookmakers would take the same view as the crowd.

The British Newspaper Library was home for the next few days, as we rifled through bygone Sporting Lifes, relentlessly researching Hole-in-One statistics and odds.

1979, we soon discovered, was not to be Ladbrokes' year at golf betting.

They had laid Benson and Hedges £8,000 to £800 (10/1) against a Hole-in-One at their prestigious tournament at St Mellion, Cornwall, but unfortunately for them the Scottish golfer Donald Armour soon obliged.

They were soon a further £40,000 down when top Japanese player and defending champion Isao Aoki aced the 155 yard 2nd in the Suntory World Matchplay championship at Wentworth.

Aoki jackpot ace is £40,000 shock for Ladbrokes

LADBROKES were £40,000 down yesterday even before they had opened for business.

At 9.15 top Japanese golfer Isao Aoki holed in one at the second in the Suntory World Match-Play Championship at Wentworth and wrecked Ladbrokes day.

They had laid building firm Bovis 40-1 to £1,000 against anyone scoring an ace at that hole during the four days of the £110,000 tournament.

Bovis had taken out the "insurance" because they were offering one of their first-floor flats over-looking the 17th green of the new Glendavon Course at Gleneagles to the first golfer to hole-in-one.

£45,000 FLAT

The flat is worth £45,000, and Aoki also receives furniture and fittings of his choice to the value of £10,000.

Defending champion Aoki picks up the richest prize offered in British golf only a year after banking the previous record, £30,000, for winning the world match-play title.

It just isn't Ladbroke's year at golf. They laid Benson and Hedges £8,000 to £800 against a hole-in-one at their big tournament at St Mellion and Scot Donald Armour obliged.

By JEREMY CHAPMAN

And they took a £70,000 hammering from the punters over Sevvy Ballesteros's victory in the Open Championship at Royal Birkdale.

Now comes the latest blow. "What a way to start work," commented director Ron Pollard wryly, "coming through the door and finding out you've just done forty grand."

The 40-1 quotation came under fire from Hills odds-maker Tommy Graham. "It seems incredibly generous," he told me. "I was approached by Bovis for the same thing and quoted them 16-1."

Graham reckons the odds against each individual shot going in the hole at the 155-yard second are around 600-1—and over the four days the 12 competitors will between them have 48 chances.

Aoki achieved his ace with a seven iron that pitched nine inches to the right of the cup and hopped in. It squared his match with Australia's David Graham, who had won the opening hole, and helped him to reach today's semi-final stage with a three and one victory.

THE SPORTING LIFE - Saturday 13th October 1979

Ron Pollard had laid the building firm Bovis 40/1 to £1,000 against any player scoring an ace at that hole during the four days of play. Although the field was limited to only 12 competitors, Pollard's assessment was branded "incredibly generous" by William Hill odds man, Tommy Graham, who when approached by the builders, would quote only 16/1.

Bovis had taken out the "insurance" because they were offering one of their first floor flats overlooking the 17th green of the new Glendavon course at Gleneagles to the first golfer to achieve a Hole-in-One.

In 1980 Coral's appeared to have got to grips with Hole-in-One betting, offering 15/8 against a single Hole-in-One and 2/5 no Hole-in-One.

> Corals reckon it's 15-8 against a hole in one being recorded over four days, and as there will be a minimum of 1,560 attempts at that feat at Gosforth's four par threes, you are certain of a good run for your money. Last year there were nine holes in one at 23 tournaments on the pro tour.
> It's 5-2 on with Corals no holes in one.

SPORTING LIFE - 3rd June 1980

'Life' reporter Jeremy Chapman considered even these odds generous, stating "If there was to be a minimum of 1560 attempts at that feat at four par threes, you are certain of a good run for your money."

> Corals were offering 15-8 against a hole-in-one this week and I was patting myself on the back for helping myself to a bit of this—until I realised that was on a loser if the feat is duplicated. Roll on Sunday!

SPORTING LIFE - 5th June 1980

Jeremy's advice proved sound. Peter Thomas, a 19 year old from Sudbury, holed out at the 197 yd tenth on the very first day. The feat was not duplicated and Corals soon found themselves coughing up.

Coral's odds-compiling skills took a nosedive in 1984. At the Lawrence Batley Golf International at the Belfry they laid a bet of £300 against any player holing in one on any of the four tournament days - at the mindbogglingly generous odds of 34/1.

Hole in one hits Corals

AMERICAN professional Danny Hepler helped himself to £1,000 and a prize motor caravan for a hole-in-one — and cost Corals £10,000.

The bookmakers had insured the motor home, supplied by B J Motor Caravans Ltd. for £300, and offered 34-1 against anyone holing in one on any of the four tournament days.

Then Hepler's two-iron shot at the 194-yards 14th bounced twice before disappearing for that jackpot ace.

Hepler is hoping to win one of ten exemptions into next week's Open Championship at St. Andrews.

THE SPORTING LIFE - July 13th 1984

This offer was taken up by B J Motors as insurance against losing the Motor Home prize they were offering. It was to be American Danny Hepler's second-day two iron shot at the 194 yard 14th hole that won him the Jackpot Prize and cost Coral's £10,000.

We noted with further interest Ken Lawrence's open diary in a July 88 edition of the Daily Star, reporting that the man from the Sporting Life, before the Open started, invested £200 at 5/1 that somebody would grab an Ace - and Wadkins contributed on the first day of the tournament.

£ANNY'S ACE!

LANNY WADKINS grabbed an ace at Lytham's par three first hole yesterday - and made a punter a packet!

The aggressive American struck a blow for the Stars and Stripes soon after David J. Russell's tee shot had hit the pin at the same hole, only to stay out by inches.

The hole-in-one gave Wadkins, who began the day two over par, a superb boost-but not as much as the man from the Sporting Life.

Before the Open started he invested £200 at 5-1 that somebody would grab an ace ... and Wadkins contributed the first of the tournament.

Sweet life
for punter

KEN LAWRENCE'S OPEN DIARY

We already knew that Hole-in-Ones were no rarity, but our research enabled us to estimate that at most European tour events the odds were no bigger than Even Money.

Destiny led us from Hole-in-One research to the distant shores of Australia in 1990.

The Aussie bookies had a reputation for laying some of the world's largest bets, and our goal had been to target the Australian Open for a Hole-in-One coup intended to obliterate the Aussie bookmaking industry for eternity.

The assault began at Melbourne's famous Flemington Park racecourse on 'Melbourne Cup' day, leading to T.A.B. betting offices and dog tracks around Melbourne, Sydney and Brisbane, followed by long drives to numerous outback racecourses, but all to no avail.

We did find one exception to the rule, top Darwin Bookmaker Brian Clark - granted special permission by the Prime Minister of Australia to quote odds on anything he chooses. Business was conducted by fax, with stakes paid directly into his Bank Account, but unfortunately the wily layer considered our request a 'hiding to nothing'!

Morale was at an all time low on that homebound flight from Sydney, with Sandy Armour's last-round Hole-in-One providing the final blow to the fruitless journey. Undeterred, we began to devise a new form of attack and discussed the possibility of a major Hole-in-One assault on the British mainland the following year.

The consequences of accepting the deadly bet were known to many, either by having already experienced the horror of a visit from us or from having been clued up by a previously stung bookie. However, we reasoned that an acceptable percentage had as yet received little or no Hole-in-One education, and we predicted a strike rate of at least one bookie in ten.

When the plane touched down at Heathrow we were convinced that 1991 would be a year the bookies would never forget.

Early access to the golf fixture list enabled us to assess five of the '91 tournaments to hold outstanding Hole-in-One possibilities. Estimating each to be Odds On, we spent the winter months in Ilford's

Public Library, photocopying the addresses of two thousand bookies from fifty volumes of the Yellow Pages. Then, with the help of street maps covering more than two hundred cities and towns, we prepared detailed itinerary sheets filling three filing cabinets to ensure optimum speed, come D-day.

By early March the plot was complete, and following the busy Cheltenham National Hunt Festival, we would commence criss-crossing Britain placing Hole-in-One bets.

This year we decided to plan one deluxe fantastic coup and really go out in style: at the conclusion of the final itinary sheet scheduled for Manchester in June, we would have visited every betting shop in England and South Wales since 1988.

Norman Schwarzkopf's Desert Storm campaign was restrained by strict rules of combat governed by UN resolutions, but fortunately for us we were not inhibited by any such embargo.

<u>Out</u> would go conventional weapons such as simply placing single bets on a suitable golf tournaments.

<u>In</u> came 'The Cluster Bomb Bet', potentially lethal, and devised to inflict maximum casualties amongst the bookmaking fraternity.

The Cluster Bomb bet consists of doubles and accumulators which allow cash to be staked against a first result. Those winnings are then risked upon the second result, and if successful, that money is staked on subsequent tournaments.

A successful tenner Hole-in-One treble landing odds of 10/1 on three golf tournaments would return a whopping £13,310.00.

Staggering odds of 1330/1, considering a treble using Hole-in-One bankers, in our view would rate little more than 4/1.

Once accepted, each successful Hole-in-One in turn would create a tidal wave of money running on to the year's final tournament for a potential pay day of all time.

Had we discovered the perfect bet and would bookies offer Hefty Odds?

THE 1991 CAMPAIGN PLAN

The U.S. OPEN, Hazeltine National, Chaska, Minnesota.
Par threes : 194yd 4th, 166yd 8th, 204yd 13th, 182yd 17th.
No men's tour event has been staged at Hazeltine since
Tony Jacklin's 1970 Open triumph, now totally redesigned
there was an absence of form. However, with play starting
at 7.00am each day, with the last 52 group out at 3.30pm,
this event could not be left from the line up.

The VOLVO PGA,
Wentworth, Surrey.
Par three's : 155yd 2nd,
191yd 5th, 186yd 10th,
164yd 14th. In 1990 there
were four Hole-in-Ones
scored in the corresponding
event, which carries the
distinction for the most
ever scored in a PGA
tournament in Great
Britian. Wentworth was
also the venue of the
famous "Aoki" house
winning ace.

THE BRITISH OPEN,
Royal Birkdale.
Par threes : 202yd 4th,
156yd 7th, 184yd 12th,
199yd 14th. The par
threes on this traditional
course boast a
true test of shorter
iron skill, but statistics
have yielded many aces
over the years.

Paying close
attention not to
stray into areas
worked the previous
year, the 1991 targets
were to be the South
Coast of England, from
Plumpton to Plymouth,
including Bristol and Bath. North to
Leicester, Nottingham, and Derby,
followed by Birmingham and surrounding districts,
which alone has four separate Yellow Pages. Sweeping
northwest through Stafford and Stoke-on-Trent to
Liverpool, Preston and Cumbria, with the Manchester region
scheduled for a July conclusion of the campaign.

THE BENSON AND HEDGES
St Mellion, Cornwall.
par threes : 185yd 4th, 140yd 8th,
202yd 11th, 174yd 14th. Formerly
held at Fulford York, the sponser
switched to the Jack Nicklaus
designed course in 1990. Although
the course coming under much
player criticism, American Steve
Bowman and Andrew Sherbourne,
were right on target holing out at
the 8th and 14th respectively and
not forgetting Mark McNulty's ace
in practice (did not count) made
this course a sure fire banker for
1991.

THE EUROPEAN OPEN,
Walton Heath, Surrey.
Par threes : 174yd 5th,
189yd 9th, 155yd 17th.
Only three short holes,
however, it would prove
very unlikely to reduce the
probability of sucess when
recalling the little white ball
had sailed obligingly into the
cup of each during recent
tournaments.

2. A MILLION POUNDS
TO A CARROT

The launch of the 1991 attack started on Monday 18th March in the Sussex town of Chichester. We had earlier stopped off at a roadside Little Chef for a bite of breakfast, but as the time approached 10.30 John was already marching into the town's Hugh Gunning betting shop. I decided to wait in the car to plan the quickest route to the next shop, but forty minutes later I was becoming anxious when he had not returned.

Past experience told me this was probably good news because John's brand of patter usually took quite a bit of time - but there was also the chance he was being throttled by a previously stung bookie. Minutes later he was back, counting a large wad of betting slips consisting of about twenty 'hole-in-one' doubles at odds of 5/1 for each golf tournament (35/1 each double).

Our elation at this fantastic start was similar to the excitement of a Yellow Disc being slotted into a Golf tournament scoreboard. This was the early bit of luck we had prayed for, because if we could continue to make steady progression by investing in the five banker events, our goal of making each double worth a fortune by St. Mellion would be bang on the cards. We left Chichester knowing we would not return until after the final banker event, the European Open at Walton Heath, had taken place in September.

Sightseeing around the South Coast of England is many people's idea of the ideal holiday and over the next few days of schlapping round the South's bookies searching for Hole-in-One odds, we had managed to increase our potential payday - if all our bankers were successful - to something in excess of £27,000.

The second bookie on Wednesday's itinerary took quite a bit of finding, but eventually Brian Striple Commissions appeared somewhere in the middle of Yonksville. The shop had the usual early morning codger brigade floating around, and as the bookie appeared oblivious to everything around him, John decided to wait for his telephone conversation to draw to a conclusion.

The wide open shirt neck, sunglasses, gold chains, watch, bracelets, rings and welcoming lopsided smile made the guy, at least in his mid forties, look like something between Elvis Presley and Liberace. John was dressed as a typical out-for-his-lunch-break office worker, but armed with £5,000 in fifties, like a Cobra he prepared to stirke. He explained that he was going to the Benson and Hedges golf tournament at St. Mellion in a couple of weeks, and although he didn't want to bet on any particular player, he did need some sort of an interest in the event and wondered if Brian could offer him odds for any player to Hole-in-One.

The old bottle always took a bit of a hammering at this point in the proceedings, because in the next few seconds the bookie's body language would reveal all. Permutations are endless, but the two most common to pick up on are a sudden rush of blood to the face telling you they have definitely been stung before so get out of the shop as quickly as possible, or a lethargic scratching of the head while mumbling, "Well, it's the first time I've heard that one, mate," encouraging you to go for the throat.

The bookie slowly broke into a smirking smile and began nodding his head. "Hole-in-One, yeah," he replied. "I remember that bet from a couple of years back." He went on to explain that a gang of blokes had actually fiddled Ladbrokes out of fortunes by somehow fixing a Hole-in-One!

John had computed in his brain that the chances of being offered Hole-in-One odds were now very slim, so the next few words came as quite a shock. "I'll lay you 33/1," he blurted, with all the confidence of the late William Hill.

"How much can I have, mate?" asked John realising through past experience he would probably say just a tenner.

"Have what you like," came the reply. "I'll lay you a twenty thousand to one if you want it, any less you can bet 33/1."

The £50,000 shop limit prominently displayed in six-inch blue letters prompted John to find out if his offer was genuine or just a bluff, so he slid into a corner and scratched out ten £40 Hole-in-One doubles using the five banker events.

John's move would be to attempt to win well in excess of the shop limit, because although it was advertised at £50,000, he had to ensure that if only one double were to prove successful a good chunk would still be won.

The bookie probably thought his stitch-up offer of only 25/1 had deterred John from having a bet, but when he returned to the counter with £440 in readies, explaining that he was going to all the major golfing events through the summer and asking for some doubles, the mathematical calculations that followed had to be seen to be believed.

"Do you know how much this bet comes to?" he asked, clearly shaken. "I can't lay this," he went on. "Each double returns twenty-five grand, that's about £1/4 million if the lot cops." John thought he'd blown it by being too bold with the stakes but when he asked if it was still OK to bet singles at 25/1, the bookie's reply was just what John wanted to hear. "That's no problem," he blurted out with renewed bravado.

John decided to slide back into his corner pitch and scratch out four £250 singles, leaving aside the US Open, which for some reason the bookie had made it clear he did not want to accept. There was no way John was going to risk blowing himself out again by going in with the lot from the kick off, so he started off by presenting the St. Mellion slip.

Brian spent the next few seconds gazing at John's clearly printed instructions, then without further fuss scratched the 25/1 odds on the slip and rang it through the till. "That's OK," came the reply as he handed back the slip.

John wasted little time in presenting the remaining slips, which were accepted now with a distinct air of caution. John's agonising funk that the slips would find their way through the shop till as quickly as possible had to wait, as each was now being carefully scrutinised in turn. A count of the stake money together with some late mental arithmetic at last prompted him to take the plunge and stick them through the till.

Clutching the carbon copies, John felt like he had just been handed the baton in the Olympic final of the men's relay and just wanted to sprint out of the shop door, but plumped instead for a simple "Thanks, mate," and casually wandered away, having created a further potential £26,000 pay day.

Parts of the South Coast had been worked in previous years, but there were still enough bookies in the Portsmouth and Southampton Yellow Pages to keep us busy until the weekend.

By Sunday night we were already driving towards the Midlands, having created an £82,000 potential payday, way beyond expectations.

Our spirits were high as we eventually approached the hotel in Castle Bromwich that was to be our base for the next several days. It had taken us absolutely ages to prepare our itinerary from the four huge volumes of Yellow Pages covering the Birmingham area where we would commence battle the next morning. However, our eagerness to get stuck into the Brummie bookies by mid afternoon suffered a severe blow as our hard work produced nothing other than disappointment. The one-bet-in-ten target we had originally set ourselves was beginning to look like one in sixty six if we were lucky.

The sickening cries from the Brummie bookie jungle of "6/4 - what's golf - William Hill - we only bet on the horses - doesn't it make you want to throw up!" - continued for several more days with only the odd £50 at 14/1 providing encouragement.

The breakthrough came as we worked our way north west towards Wolverhampton when we first caught sight of the betting office owned by 'Terry Turner.' John thought the elderly guy behind the counter was a good Two On chance to be the owner, wandered over to ask if he had any prices for the St. Mellion golf tournament yet. "You'll have to ask Kid. He'll be back in a few minutes," came the reply.

Leaving it behind on this occasion the boardman continued the delicate business of distributing betting slips around the premises. John perched himself on a stool, enduring the unwelcome advances of a long haired nutter begging him to have his b!?*?+ks on trap 6 in the afternoon first race at Monmore.

Just minutes later the happy go lucky figure of Terry Turner strolled past clutching a newspaper containing fish and chips, and made his way behind the counter. A young clean-cut sort of a guy, he appeared to be very approachable as John began his standard "I'm going to the golf in a few weeks time," spiel, but when he responded by saying that some bookies were offering odds of 16/1 for a Hole-in-One last year, John knew he was in with some sort of a chance. He then merrily picked up the phone, saying he needed to speak to a mate of his before quoting odds.

"Hello, Pete," the conversation began. "We did used to lay 16/1 on the hole-in-one bet, didn't we?"

The sudden danger of a revised 6/4 quote fortunately did not materialise, as Pete reassured Terry the 16/1 odds had indeed been laid - clearly by a bookie Terry had previously worked for. John was not the least surprised to hear his previous employer had been offering those big 16/1 odds because throughout the previous three years, not only the minnows but many of the big bookmaking chains had also been quoting generous Hole-in-One odds.

"Yes, that's OK, I'll lay you 16/1," he then eagerly said as John sensed he was keen to take a bet. "Golfer, are you?" he continued.

"Yes, I go to all the golf tournaments and this sort of bet gives me a cheap interest," replied John. "How much can I have on?" John was ready to grab as much of that 16/1 as he could lay his hands on.

"Anything you want," he boldly replied, not realising John would be only too pleased to take his words literally if given the chance.

The important factor here was not to frighten him off with enormous stakes, so John decided to ask if he could bet £50 at 16/1 in the season's first event at St. Mellion in Cornwall. "No problem," Tel confidently replied as he scratched the odds on the slip and rang the bet through the till.

"If it's OK with you, I might as well have the same bet on the rest of the golf events I'll be going to," John boldly asked, ensuring the St. Mellion slip was buried deep in his trouser pocket.

"Absolutely no problem - by the way, where's the British Open this year?" Terry enthused, keen to get his hands on a few more readies.

"Royal Birkdale," John replied, making his way towards the betting slips. In addition to the three singles, he decided to try his luck with a little Cluster Bet, and quickly scratched out the four events on a separate slip, mixing them up with six £5.00 Hole-in-One doubles.

The telephone rang before John had been given the chance to sort out the readies, and he dreaded the possibility of a late 'nause' entering the proceedings. To John's relief, Terry retained his smile, and John allowed his stomach a couple of seconds to settle, then took his slips over to the counter.

"Are the bets O.K.?" asked John, seeking reassurance. "Sure, no problem," he sparked. "I'll even offer you 20/1 for the British Open, because I have an idea it's a difficult course."

"I've included a few fiver doubles, is that all right?" asked John, praying to the gods that he would say yes. "No problem, have what you want," he replied, already enthusiastically ringing each slip through the till.

The singles alone - if all four obliged - returned £3,600 with a possible £10,000 return from the doubles also on the cards. He stood to do his absolute cobblers.

Frustration at traffic lights changed to elation as we sped away with our collection of Terry Turner Hole-in-One betting slips complete.

The bad news was that our scheduled itinerary for the rest of the day was now in tatters because with Terry probably already on the telephone to other local bookies, explaining how some mug from London had earlier walked in to make his bottle donation to the Terry Turner benevolent fund, news of our presence in the area would probably already be spreading like wildfire.

Terry was the only bookie to lay a bet on the North West Birmingham itinerary and he had appeared out of a mass of 6/4 quotes. A telephone call from Turner to another local bookie conditioned to quote short odds could result in very serious repercussions, so we decided to make our way to Kidderminster, some fifteen miles away.

The time was already approaching 5.40 p.m. as our most productive day yet was drawing to a close, the highlights being ten £10 doubles at odds of 8/1 each banker tournament, with a late £100 single at 33/1 for St. Mellion also in the bin. We began to head back to the hotel when John remembered that about a mile or so down the road there was a bookie he had called on a few days ago, who had asked him to call back because he was about to shoot off to Worcester races.

He had promised he would have a word with the Hills rep. during the afternoon and try to get him to quote odds but with most of the racecourse reps already well clued up, John thought that poking his head around the shop door would achieve little more than completing the South West Birmingham itinerary sheet.

The Boomerang racing shop was still open for business as John entered betting shop number 18, with the bookie busy completing the final phase of the day's activities by pulling the sporting papers from the walls. He looked a little like Nigel Mansell due to his deluxe moustache, but the Adolf Hitler fringe and shifty eyes still made him look every inch a bookie.

There was clearly little time to muck about so John crashed in and asked if he had managed to get hold of a Hole-in-One price. "Oh yeah, I remember," he replied, continuing with his chores.

"I did ask around, you probably think it's a 1,000/1 shot but I'm afraid to say - (John thought, here comes the old 6/4 stakes) - it's only a 10/1 chance according to the club pro at the Belfry. I know it's not much good to you," he continued, shrugging his shoulders, "you probably don't even want to have a bet now."

Renewed with a strange surge of energy while trying to look as disappointed as possible, John realised that Boomerang was a potential target for the Cluster Bomb. "I can't believe 10/1 - that's no good to me, not 10/1," he mumbled, shaking his head in disbelief.

Frothing to Get On, but not wanting to arouse suspicion, John sat on a stool to begin an analysis of the Life's Hall Green evening dog card pinned to the wall. Minutes later the shop broom was buzzing around his legs, delivering the message that it was time to go home. "Is there any chance of betting Hole-in-One doubles at 10/1 each tournament so at least I've got some sort of chance to nick a few quid?" John asked, breaking the uncomfortable silence.

"I don't see why not," replied Nigel, sounding surprised at the pending donation.

Grabbing a handful of betting slips with his right hand while pulling his battered Golf World magazine tournament fixture list out of his rear pocket with the left, John frantically began to scratch out seven Hole-in-One doubles, mixing the banker events.

"Is it all right to have a few thirty quid doubles?"

he asked the amicable Nigel, who had now decided to sit himself down.

"That's fine, no problem," he replied. "You obviously like a bet on the golf, then?" he enthusiastically inquired.

"I usually end up laying out a few quid on match and group bets, but this hole-in-one thing just gives me a extra interest," John replied while scribbling out the British Open/European Open Double.

The quandary of when he should stop writing ended at slip seven, because despite continued encouragement from the Nigel Mansell boatometer, John was not prepared to venture out of the safety zone. "That's all I want to lose," John jokingly told him extracting five fifty pound notes from his wad of readies.

"Great," he replied, already dashing towards the cash till, clearly unable to believe his good fortune. Thirty seconds into desk-top calculation he dared to inform John that each double worked out at 120/1 if successful. He keenly pushed over seven carbon copies but was then forced into a flush as he scrambled through the payout drawer attempting to scrape up the change.

One crisp five pound note and fourteen one pound coins later, John decided to continue with the assault and promptly commenced Phase II.

"I know it's getting a bit late," asked John, probing for a positive response. Nigel's gleeful smile prompted him to continue, "but it is possible to have a few more doubles?".

"Too late, of course not, have what you like," replied Nigel, struggling to conceal his elation.

John spent what must have been a good twenty minutes mixing up the five banker events in more £30 doubles. Then with the help of his priceless tournament fixture list, he permed each banker in turn with every other suitable golf tournament on the calendar. Luckily, John had been left alone to write out the second phase of doubles, but when the completed betting slips and stake money eventually found their way to the counter top, Nigel wasted little time in lunging out of his chair to count the readies before completing the hectic bet-taking session.

Poor old Nigel had really taken the bait, but deciding to go for the Jackpot prize of an early September presentation of the shop keys, John asked if he could quickly scratch out a final six doubles. "You can have as many as you like," came his bold reply. "Whatever I don't want I'll hedge off with William Hill in the morning."

The fail safe button would now have to be switched on, because having earlier clocked the shop payout limit, the point had been reached where laying out too much stake money would reduce the value of our bets.

It was massive Odds On Nigel hadn't bothered to consult with anyone about Hole-in-One odds and he was simply indulging in one of many favourite bookmaker's games called 'Rip the punter off', convinced he would encounter few problems in hedging John's doubles elsewhere at monster odds.

(If he were able to hedge each double, let's say at 1,200/1, he would only be using ten per cent of the stake money to cover the bets and would then simply bin the rest.)

Nigel was soon ringing John's absolutely final half dozen doubles through the till and the stake money was disappearing faster than chips at a roulette table.

John reflected on the spring of 1990 when William Hill quoted odds of 5/4 for any named Hole-in-One double. Nigel would have about as much chance of getting out of this lot tomorrow morning as Bernard Manning would have of winning the men's singles title at Wimbledon.

Overjoyed at his late evening windfall, Nigel breathlessly escorted John to the door, explaining how much he was looking forward to monitoring the golf during the coming months and what a fantastic interest they now both had.

The Bandit had been waiting patiently in the car all this time, but he was quickly clued up to our further success the minute John's ecstatic boat and a fresh wad of betting slips reappeared inside the car. On a day that had increased the potential winning from £50,000 to £145,000, our target figure was progressing along like the Vegas Megabucks Pool.

We had ensured that every single bookie listed in each Yellow Pages had been seen, and our persistence at playing the numbers game was at last really beginning to pay off.

The depressing echoes of 6/4 were now forgotten as we began our early evening drive north to the Nottingham Post House, which would be our base for the next few weeks while we sorted out the bookies in the next targeted areas of Nottingham, Leicester and Derby.

The next morning we were blasted out of our beds by a 6.30 a.m. alarm call and less than an hour later we were both seated around the breakfast table. In the midst of a sea of suits, ties, Telegraphs and Daily Mails, the sudden presence of the Sporting Life began to raise a few eyebrows. Unperturbed, we carefully scrutinised each page. We left the hotel complete with briefcase, surrounded by businessmen who had no idea what we were up to. Nor could they ever have guessed.

Due to the complexity of central Derby we were using a large scale 'A to Z' street map with each bookmaker ringed so that we could easily follow the quickest route to each shop. We arrived at the first bookie, just outside the town centre, at around 10.15 a.m. As was fairly common in this part of the world, he was not due to open until 11.00 a.m. so we spent the next half hour giving the racing papers a quick and unexpected second workout. About

11.30 a.m. the lights inside the shop flickered on, so we knew the day's activities were about to start. As John entered the shop with a Sporting Life tucked under his arm, the owner - who looked more like a farmer than a bookmaker - was busy pinning the day's racing cards from the Sporting Life on to the wall, without a care in the world.

A large percentage of his customers were no doubt regular faces, so not surprisingly when a stranger appears on the scene he is treated either with extreme caution or considered a potential mug. As was always standard practice, John's role of looking around the shop in a manner the owner would hopefully associate with that of an inexperienced or mug punter would now be acted out. Casually, John told him about looking forward to travelling to Cornwall in a few weeks' time to watch the country's first big golf event, the Benson and Hedges tournament. Although John did not really want to bet on a particular player to win, could he possibly offer odds for any player to score Hole-in-One to add a bit of interest throughout the four days? His smile changed to a frown and he barked, "You won't get any odds for that round here, mate!"

John's move now was to soft-talk his way out of this: clearly the bookie had either been 'stung' in the past or was already clued up to the odds, so he was told of a magazine article about Hole-in-Ones, and asked if there were any odds associated with it. He replied, "You won't get a bet like that round here, mate. Every bookie I know has either already been done or knows it's Odds On."

If John's acting had not so far been Oscar-winning material, he would already have been escorted out of his shop. A quick thankyou, and he returned to the car. He told me that we could well be in for a bad day, as it seemed likely the area was already clued up but, undaunted, we set off again.

After another five shops brought a similar response from grim-faced bookies, we found ourselves outside the Stable Street betting shop of Arthur Whittaker. Nothing so far that morning had given us any clue that this little corner betting shop situated in the back streets of Derby was to change both our lives dramatically and would reshape our destinies.

I parked the car in a nearby side road and without any need to exchange words, John jumped out and made the short uphill walk to the shop door. His first sight was of TV screens displaying various odds available on afternoon horse races and other sporting events. A young bearded man sat behind a very restrictive glass security screen which made communication virtually impossible unless your head was at right angles. The beard was serving an old man sporting a Campbell tartan cloth cap, and so to save a great deal of awkward explaining through the glass screen I wrote out the bet. Pushing the betting slip under his counter, he asked what odds were available for any player to score a Hole-in-One in the forthcoming Benson and Hedges golf tournament. After consulting a number of pages on his monitor screen with no apparent success, he stared at John, and to his total astonishment said, "One hundred to one."

A sudden shiver of excitement went down John's spine. Realising the unexpected potential of the situation John asked him if he would accept a bet of £50. He replied, "Have what you like." He wrote the 100/1 odds on the slip and rang it through the shop till. Trusting that his luck would continue, John asked if he would accept the same bet for both the Volvo PGA tournament and the British Open, also to take place later in the year. He confidently replied, "That's OK."

John knew it was massive Odds On that at least one of the bets would show a substantial profit, so a return visit to the premises would be almost inevitable. He quickly computed in his mind what price the double of landing leg one, 'getting on,' and leg two, actually getting paid out, then pointed out, "These are large odds you've laid me: if they're successful they'll come to a considerable amount of money." "Nothing to worry about. Once we lay odds they can't be altered," John was assured as the young beard pointed to the shop £25,000 limit.

"Your bets would only return fifteen grand, so there's no problem," he continued, "but if you want more on you'll have to come back and ask Mr Whittaker." In the circumstances, keeping a cool head was an absolute 'must'. John knew full well he was monster Odds On for a deluxe payday, and wanted nothing more than to get out of the shop quickly, but the last thing he needed was to arouse suspicion by rushing to 'Get On'. So John said, "These bets will be fine," and casually added, "See you later," as he made his way to the door.

He sprinted to the car like Carl Lewis.

"What happened?" I asked, anticipating good news.

"The St Mellion bet, and the same for the Volvo and British Open," John feverishly panted, waving his flush of Whittaker betting slips under my nose.

His breathless enthusiasm continued for a good ten minutes but the implications of the bets had to be discussed. We knew Arthur Whittaker would soon return from lunch and would probably waste little time in phoning other local bookmakers to warn them we were in the area. As this would mean no warm smile of welcome from the other bookies on our list, we decided to take emergency action.

I grabbed the file for a town twenty five miles away, put the car into gear and we set off. Judging from what we had learned from various grim-faced bookies that morning, it seemed Odds On that Arthur Whittaker was in for a very nasty shock! We imagined the scene: Mr Whittaker returning to his shop after a pleasant lunch and asking the manager how things had gone while he had been out; the reply that he'd done really well as some guy had laid out £165 on some mug bets; eagerly showing the betting slips, expecting praise for his initiative ... and two seconds later finding himself dialling 999 for emergency services - requiring all three to 'come at once!'

We felt we were now a good distance from the

disaster area. It was Odds On that Arthur had sent out the ▐ WANTED ▌ posters with myself fitting the description, so with a bounty on John's head we decided to switch roles: the real 'Bandit' could slip into action. My completely different style of attack would involve acting out the flamboyant mug punter. Blasting my way into a bookie, instantly blurting out to everyone within earshot that I had been doing my absolute cobblers, I would then go on to enthuse that I had 'had it off' the previous evening at the dogs and while counting a large wad of readies, I would then approach the wide eyed bookie. This worked well: the bookies would think this was easy money, and would give me the advantage of getting large stakes on with my educated accent and smart-but-casual appearance.

We parked the car and treated ourselves to a cup of coffee and a roll. I was hyping myself up for the first call of the campaign which was very reminiscent of Hulk Hogan saying, "We'll show our little puntermaniacs what we're made of!" and I strutted off, full of confidence, to face the enemy.

The bookie with the prominent red bow tie stood at the other end of the long, narrow shop. I decided to show exaggerated interest in the afternoon's racing activities and gazed for some time at the current odds available for a number of forthcoming sports events. I was aware that I was being clocked by the owner so I decided to approach him. He was smartly dressed - a typical bookmaker - short and stocky with a jolly red face . As I neared the counter he welcomed me with a smile and the unexpected words, "I know you!". Confused, my mind immediately started searching for a clue, my first thoughts being that John had somehow picked up the wrong file and we had ventured into an area which had possibly been worked the previous year. This called for emergency action. The flamboyant punter image would have to be given an enforced rest as I brought to life a new character with a friendly, enquiring attitude.

I asked him what odds were available for Spurs to win the FA Cup. He dialled three digits on the small monitor in front of him, then told me I could have 7/1. I then asked if he could obtain odds for Nick Faldo to win the Benson and Hedges golf tournament. With his eyes working overtime looking through the pages he said, "They have only got the odds for Faldo to win the US Masters, and he's 8/1."

I replied, "I'm going to the tournament for a weekend break, and I wanted a bet to give me an interest." When he suggested that I come back 'nearer the event', I asked him whether he could quote me a price for any player to score a Hole-in-One. Startled, and rocking backwards, he said, "I knew it was you. You asked me for the same bet last year!" His red face creased with laughter and it was some time before he could compose himself. He evidently found difficultly in choosing his next words but eventually stuttered through his laughter, "A bookmaker in Derby earlier today laid three bets at a hundred to one, was it you who stitched him up?" I looked him in the eye and with a chuckle said, "Definitely not!"

"This bookie in Derby stands to do his cobblers," said Red Bow Tie cheerfully.

"How come?" I asked, pumping for information.

"When he phoned me it was difficult to understand his babble, but I do know he stands to do an absolute chunk!" he replied.

He went on to say that the Derby bookmaker had been frantically phoning other bookies trying to hedge the bets to no avail, and then broke into a second bout of uncontrollable laughter. Realising that the Whittaker phone calls, going out like the waves of an Atom Bomb mushroom spreading from Derby, had already reached out twenty five miles, and that my quest was now a lost cause, I asked, jokingly, "No chance of the hundreds with you then?" to which he replied, "I've got a feeling you've caused enough mischief for one day already!" With my hand on the doorhandle I shouted back, "Is there any chance of betting anything at under the odds then?" to which there was no reply, only the fading echoes of his laughter.

John, waiting in the local tearooms and midway through his third cup of coffee, was surrounded by old ladies enjoying their afternoon tea and scones. As he looked out of the small quaint windows he saw me approaching with the grin still on my face and as soon as I was inside asked, "How'd it go?" "Whittaker's gone off his rocker and he's been phoning everywhere trying to hedge the bets. I think we'd better call it a day - anyway it's 3.30 pm," I replied.

As we drove back to our temporary mission control

at Nottingham, we were both on a high, knowing we had achieved our week's target in one day - not to mention the work down South - which now added up to over £150,000 in just four days.

"We're both on a roller coaster that's out of control, it's heading towards the centre of the earth, there's a pot of gold on the other side, we'll be blasting through Australia before we know where we are, nothing can stop us now!"

These results were motivating us even further but by the time we had arrived at our hotel I had managed to calm down. We felt slightly guilty about knocking off so early, because our goal was to work every day without a break until the last shop had closed. Once in the hotel room, our first job was to organise ourselves ready for the next day. Due to the unforeseen Whittaker scenario I said, "I think we had better head south to Leicester and then make our way back up to Nottingham." Reaching for my briefcase, which was as cherished as the Chancellor's, I carefully tucked away the Arthur Whittaker vouchers, removed the Leicester file and spread the large-scale map and the local 'A to Z' street directory on the bed. "We've got twenty eight calls on this file, and if all goes well we should cover this in a day or so," I said, and proceeded to pinpoint the first victim on the map.

Gasping for refreshment, we then headed to the bar for a couple of cold beers to celebrate the day's success. "Whey hey! stitch up!" was the Bandit's response to a charge of £4.80 for two lagers.

After indulging in a deluxe chicken tikka we returned to the bar, which was now bustling with sales reps.

"'Sales meetings ... I'd never want to be part of that nightmare scene again!" I blurted as we perched ourselves on two stools by the bar. The air was unpleasantly thick with cigar smoke and it was difficult to hear ourselves speak above the din.

The guy sitting next to me was tailor made for the scene, wearing business attire, with scotch in hand and a magnum moustache for good measure. Apparently mistaking us for fellow employees he asked what time the company's annual sales conference was to begin in the morning. "We work for a company which holds one-day sheepskin and leather coat sales at different hotels throughout the country," was my reply, to save the usual lengthy explanations regarding our true activities.

Energised by alcohol, the rep described how he enjoyed being a member of a big team and liked the security of a large company with all its benefits. "Well, the car's thrown in, the petrol's paid, and it's a cushy old number really, if you play your cards right," we were then assured.

Knowing the sales rep's scene only too well and having nearly suffered a nervous breakdown the last time round, slowly my memory drifted back to the down side of a previous existence, which had motivated us to get stuck into the Hole-in-One game in the first place ...

3. A SPELL OF WORK THERAPY

... As John entered the Maltster's Arms, "It's all right for you in Coral's," I bluntly told him. "I almost died of hypothermia at Hackney Wick's Dogs this afternoon, and went through the card without backing a winner," I despondently spluttered."If I carry on bumming around much longer I'll end up skint. Cosmetics is the game - I'll be on to those employment agencies again in the morning," I mumbled on, reluctantly resigning myself to a spell of work therapy. Getting a job quickly called for emergency measures.

With a carefully constructed CV, I attended numerous interviews for the purpose of desensitising myself to the ordeal, so that when a worthwhile position came along my performance would be worthy of an Oscar. On this occasion my choice was the vacant position of sales representative covering the East London and Essex area for a well-known cosmetics company. Thanks to my impeccable credentials, I found myself as predicted amongst the last six contenders, sitting in the waiting room with five minutes to go. I was full of confidence with turbo-chargers at the ready, excited by the challenge of scheming myself into yet another job and beating all contenders. I took a final glance at my deluxe CV to ensure I would not come a cropper under the rigours of this final interrogation.

Geoffrey Hayden, the South of England Sales Manager, opened the door and welcoming me with a warm smile, said, "Paul, come on in." I was introduced to the company's UK Manager from Texas, Mr Peter Serrin, who reminded me of a typical American TV quiz show host, complete with sparkling choppers. Formalities over, I was invited to take a seat.

"Before we proceed with the interview," he said, "we would like to explain to you exactly what this position would involve. You would be working the East London and Essex area as a sales representative on a very attractive remuneration: a brand new Cavalier car plus other company benefits including our excellent pension plan." Looking directly into my eyes, he continued.

"To be frank with you, Paul, we need a person with very special qualities. We need someone with a first class proven track record, ideally in the FMCG field. He must also have the skills, drive and dedication to fill the shoes of the now promoted Freddie Phillips." Looking very serious, his voice deepening, he went on.

"Paul, if we entrusted this most prestigious position to you, you would have a lot to live up to." He concluded, "So, Paul, that's us. Now let's hear a bit about you - let's go through your career."

Thanks to having thoroughly memorised my CV, the answers were about to flow. Knowing that an unblemished reference was on standby if required, I explained that I had previously enjoyed over five years working in the cosmetics industry. I went on to say that for the past eight years I had worked for a very well known FMCG company and that I was their top sales executive, covering the North London and East Anglia area. The previous rep had, for some reason, become disillusioned and had been asked to leave, so, I confessed, the opportunity for impressive results was already there. Within the space of two years, I told them, I had more than quadrupled the previous annual sales figures for the area, and one year later, at the company's annual sales conference, I had been awarded the honour of 'Sales Executive of the Year' and presented with an inscribed plaque and a two-week all-expenses-paid trip to Istanbul. Since then, I continued, I had had many more successful years with the company.

Geoff asked the inevitable question, "Why did you leave?" I told him that I had by far the most extensive area in the company to look after, which had meant me spending numerous nights away from home. I then went on to explain that I was very much looking forward to settling down in the very near future to marry my fiancee who herself had worked since she left college for a well known High Street bank (knowing these type of companies prefer their staff to be associated with stable people, not someone like myself).

I could tell that both Peter and Geoffrey were impressed by what they were hearing, and I felt I was now reaching the peak of my performance. Geoffrey asked, "Can you please tell us in a few words why we should employ you." Confidently I replied: "Well you've just heard that I've only held four positions to date, all with major blue chip companies. I was with my last company for just over eight years and my record in that time, I feel sure you'll both agree, speaks for itself. Before that I enjoyed five marvellous years with another well known cosmetics company very similar to yourselves and enjoyed the environment immensely. Going way back, my career started with selling various soft goods door-to-door on credit. This died an instant death when the major banks sent out credit cards to all their customers. I feel absolutely certain that this tough grounding gave me the skills and confidence needed to lay a sound foundation for the rest of my selling career."

Peter interrupted. "What sort of things did you sell, and what did you say?"

"Would you like me to demonstrate?" I asked. After murmurings during a mini conference between the pair, they agreed. I asked if I could briefly leave the room so that I could re-enact my standard entrance. "Sure!" replied Peter, his shining choppers sparkling in the reflection of the fluorescent lights.

I stood up, feeling distinctly uncomfortable in this unaccustomed suit and longing for my normal attire, straightening the ex-public school tie I had recently acquired from Harrods specially for the occasion. My mind was now running wild with mischievous ideas, and I chose one of my favourite selling scams from my vast repertoire. With my turbos fully charged, I knocked on the door, heard a relaxed 'Come in,' and burst in, bouncing violently up and down doing my silly walk. To a look of total astonishment on their faces, I said "Good morning, madam. They've just sent me round from Hugo Walker's, now I'll just tell you what's happened, about three weeks ago we got a large number of long-haired acrylic rugs from our manufacturer but they've only been sent through to our local branch in four colours. Now if by any chance you happen to need a long haired acrylic rug and provided you don't mind having red, tangerine, purple or blue, we're doing them as a special offer, they normally retail in the catalogues at £13.95. We're doing them today at cost price which is £6.95, the only bad news is that no one house in the road is allowed to buy more than two. Now you can either pay cash or we do them for fifty pence deposit then fifty pence a week for one or a pound deposit then a pound a week for two, there's absolutely no credit charge whatsoever and the man calls round every Thursday. The other man came round about a week ago and I know most of your neighbours have already bought one, but if you were out and haven't had a chance of seeing them before, can I show them to you?"

I walked across the room with my imaginary acrylic rugs tucked firmly under my arm, still vigorously bouncing up and down and continuing my silly walk. Out of the corner of my eye I could see Peter and Geoff looking clearly amused. Totally absorbed, and reliving a memorable page from my past, I threw the imaginary rugs on to the floor inches from their feet, then stroking one as though it were a priceless pedigree cat, I reached for my order book, looked directly at Peter and said, "Is it one or two you're after? And your name is Mrs ...?"

Somewhat out of breath I flopped back into my chair, and could see Geoff and Peter whispering and nodding approvingly to each other.

Geoff, now deciding to adopt a very business-like manner, said, "Paul, we have both been very impressed by the way you have interviewed, and although we are not in a position to officially confirm your appointment at present, we will most certainly be telephoning you at home sometime during the afternoon to let you know how you got on."

I left, feeling so confident that I would not have hesitated in betting Five On paying ten pence in the pound betting tax given half a chance! Just after 4.00 pm the phone rang as expected. I was in the process of folding away my Harrods tie when I was greeted by the enthusiastic and now familiar voice of Geoff on the line. "You interviewed very well this morning, Paul, and I can now officially welcome you to the company." With exaggerated excitement I replied, "Thanks very much." Geoff went on to explain that the company's annual sales conference was to take place at the Belfry Golf Club near Birmingham in eight days' time and he felt that this would be an opportune place and time for me to meet the team. I would also be required, he explained, to attend a one-day induction course immediately after the conference. He concluded by telling me that I would be receiving written confirmation of my conditions of employment together with maps and documentation relevant to the sales conference within the next day or so.

During the intervening eight days my enthusiasm for this new appointment had already begun to wane, especially when I considered the possible consequences in the light of my past exploits in similar positions. I arrived at the Belfry and was forced to park my car a good hundred yards from the front entrance due to the car park being tightly packed with 1.6 Vauxhall Cavaliers. I trudged through the snow ... *remembering a previous fine summer's day watching Seve Ballesteros, just one stroke clear, strutting up the famous eighteenth fairway with me firmly clutching a betting voucher confirming my bet of five monkeys, running through the crowd like catweazel to gain an optimum view of his forthcoming second shot* ... to a conference hall I had never before realised existed.

The old bottle was now twitching as I made my way through a lounge packed full of unfamiliar faces. I kept an eye out for Geoff as I sat down at one of the tables and poured myself a cup of coffee, surrounded by dozens of smooth, well-dressed men and women sitting in tightly packed islands around the lounge. One enthusiastic boat with the confidence of Bruce Forsyth said, "You're a new face here?" Like a lamb I replied, "Yes. I'm taking over Freddie Phillips' area." He fired back, "Top Man: just been promoted, I understand. I hear they had a difficult job replacing him."

Concerned by these last few words I nervously checked my watch, realising that, but for my bloomer, I would now be making my way to Paddington Station to catch the Newbury Racecourse Special, on which the topic of conversation would be the afternoon's racecard and not, as I could overhear, the enthusiastic banter of the sales reps saying, "How did your canvas go?" and, "I'm afraid I didn't reach my target, old boy." I knew this was not my scene and that I was definitely not going to be equal to the occasion!

In reality, my last job, at a men's shop in Romford, had lasted only three days before I 'packed it in' due to an allergic dust reaction to just about every duty I was asked to perform. The final crunch came when I was handed a 'Mr Sheen' container complete with duster! This experience was over a year ago, and still reflecting on this memorable episode, I found myself being ushered into a large conference hall, and felt like I was about to be thrown to the gladiators in the arena. I started to fumble with my itinerary sheet, frantically searching for my seat number which I eventually found, with my name embossed in large gold capital letters on a plush looking card attached to the backrest.

As the noise of shuffling chairs died down, Sue - the attractive bubbly blonde spokeswoman - took the rostrum. She was greeted with loud applause and one rather out-of-place late wolf-whistle. Faced with a slide projector and surrounded by a mini cinema screen, she announced into the microphone in well-modulated tones, "Well, how quickly the time has gone since our last meeting only a year ago! And now, without any further ado, let's hear a few words from our advertising manager Pete Longhurst!" Pete, with a large grin, catapulted himself on stage and said, "Thank you Sue. Hello again everybody, I'll be giving you all details of our very exciting forthcoming TV campaign and our new retail outlet promotion packages ....." After about twenty minutes without coming up for breath, his show drew to a close. Sue, on stage once more, said, "Thanks Pete. Now it's over to our special guest, our marketing supremo Mr John Webster!" He duly unveiled a multitude of charts and graphs which showed more lines than Clapham Junction, and waving his ruler like a conductor's baton, he proceeded to pinpoint the company's main competitors. After a further barrage from Geoff, his great rival Jack Green, the northern regional Sales Manager, took the rostrum. Although no-one could understand a single word with him seemingly doing an impersonation of Lester Piggot, this did not deter him from speaking for twice as long as anyone else.

I vaguely remembered entering a third hour of waffle when I was roused by a sudden loud burst of applause as the European Sales Manager suddenly stormed in like Norman Schwarzkopf, complete with notes in hand.

Towards the end of his lengthy speech I was abruptly brought to attention when he said, "We have two new family members with us since we last met. The first being Christine who will cover the South Wales area, and a new man who I must confess really did take a great deal of finding." As I looked round the packed hall I could see many darkened faces nodding their heads in approval.

He continued, "As you know, Freddie has been
with the company for over thirty years and is
known to most of you personally. His recent promotion required an extensive search to find a suitable replacement, but after interviewing well in
excess of five hundred applicants in three rounds
of interviews we were lucky enough to find Paul,"
adding, "Would the two new family members please
stand up."

Throughout the past hour my mind had been
fixed only on the forthcoming Benson and Hedges
snooker draw. I staggered to my feet and forced
myself to attention, praying to the gods that I was
not going to be called upon to make a speech. He
went on, "Would all of you please wish the two of
them the very best of luck." To football crowd
applause from the highly charged executives I
looked round the room with an embarrassed smile.

The ensuing scene made me feel like I was a member of the cast in the riotous end of the Muppet Show. I now knew without doubt that I was an impostor in the camp!

After a none-too-pleasant lunch, with sales talk still echoing in my ears, and bent over with acute indigestion, I now had the pleasures of the afternoon's sales meeting to look forward to. This was to be conducted by the Southern Regional Sales Manager, my new boss Geoff.

I took my seat at the horseshoe arrangement of desks and nervously fumbled with my pencil as I glanced at Geoff. He was all smiles as he presented me with a large new briefcase saying, "It includes our special leather backed employee instruction manual." With a forced look of glee on my face I once again took my seat, bewildered by the multitude of books and forms in front of me. Geoff said, reassuringly, "Well, Paul, you're new here, so don't worry too much about the afternoon's proceedings as all will be explained to you at your induction on Monday." Thinking that it would need to be at least a week long to sort that lot out, realised as the afternoon progressed that this was only the tip of the iceberg. I hoped that my newly acquired briefcase had a very strong handle, as Geoff, in full sales pitch, was handing out a never-ending stream of different coloured forms which the other sales reps were eagerly accepting and meticulously stacking in piles. Sipping my water at regular intervals with Geoff's words of wisdom going in one ear and out the other, the nightmare eventually drew to a close with my head spinning so much that I would not have been able to tell a damaged goods pad from a daily report book!

Geoff, looking as sprightly and fresh as when first seen that morning, said, "You all might as well leave your papers where they are. I'll either see you in the bar later, or bright and early in the morning." I thought to myself, "I'm really going to cop it here."

After a very confused evening and a still unexplained nightmare, we were up early the next morning for breakfast. I felt naked at the table without my Sporting Life and Racing Post, and was forced to endure the other sales reps' chatter about how much they were looking forward to Day Two. How my feelings had changed from the time I had left my interview and had driven home singing, 'Oh what a smart arse I am!' Trying to look as keen as anyone, but definitely feeling in need of psychiatric care, I made sure that I was first into the meeting room. Geoff, busily preparing his instruments of torture like Vincent Price, greeted me cheerfully. Overnight, stacks of boxes had appeared. I said to Geoff, "There's not much room in here now with all these boxes. And why have I got about twenty more than anybody else?" He replied that they included all my record cards, instore product promotional displays, emergency repair kits for damaged cosmetics dispensers, a product display manual and one dozen boxes each containing a complete set of lipstick testers.

As I wobbled to my seat, Geoff added that we would start the morning by discussing the new promotion for this canvass. Slowly the onslaught of new red promotion order pads, damaged product return pads and discontinued stock credit refund pads were piling up in front of us. When we stopped for our allotted one hour's lunch, my pile of forms and boxes would have been a challenge even for Chris Bonington to climb. Geoff said enthusiastically, "Due to our workload, can we resume in about twenty five minutes?"

Staggering from the room, hoping that a cup of coffee would revive me, I was now so far gone that even the thought of doing my cobblers at Hackney Dogs would have been ecstasy!

'Deadly Nightshade' was the crackpot name given to a new eyeshadow and mascara promotion kit. Geoff, after much enthusing over this new masterpiece, distributed the relevant literature to each one of us in turn. Up till now, my only sign of joining in the happy party had been knowledgeable silent nods of appreciation: these had become apparent to all concerned, who were no doubt expecting as promised the new injection of wealth and knowhow that the area desperately needed, from the top man on this occasion- namely myself. As Geoff's wild eyes scanned the room for volunteers, I tried to look invisible - but in vain. Geoff said, "Paul, you've heard what I said, show the others here how our new superstar performs." My only consolation was the five thousand pounds I had just won on my imaginary insurance bet of twenty thousand at Fours On against such a catastrophe!

As I slowly made my way to join Geoff at the front of the room, all eyes were on me in expectation of a performance worthy of Olivier. Geoff said, "All we need now is an obstinate Mr Singh to be the chemist proprietor. How about you, Keith?" Now I knew I was in trouble. Keith, probably envious of my build-up and supposedly impeccable credentials, leapt from his seat. Clearly a highly charged executive, he had been the most productive member of the meeting. Dressed immaculately, with a powder-white complexion and well-groomed hair, he reminded me of a professional snooker player with the killer look of Steve Davis.

I frantically scoured the plastic pages of my product display manual, desperately searching for the insert displaying the dark colours and shades of 'Deadly Nightshade' which would shortly be let loose on the country's countless Mr Singhs. With trembling fingers and soggy armpits, I eventually found the page. Keith was now smirking and sensing that I was already <u>all at sea:</u> the performance which followed is best described as 'Classic Frank Spencer'. Geoff's look of happy contentment had now turned to mild concern, hoping it was a minor hiccup rather than a sign of things to come!

I retreated to the safety of my seat, still reeling with embarrassment and wondering if this performance was better than my legendary hygiene kit fiasco of a few years back. The room had suddenly become silent. Geoff interrupted "Let's move right along; two more volunteers, please."

As the afternoon dragged on, I was now checking my watch every few minutes as 5 pm slowly approached, and thinking, 'Thank God I'll soon be away.' Geoff, still looking as fresh as a daisy, said with the renewed energy of Popeye after swallowing a can of spinach, "It's Question Time!" I could not believe the sight as hands were thrust skywards. After the initial questions were answered, Geoff slowly grilled each one of us in turn to ensure that everyone was ready for the first day of the new canvass on Monday morning. When my turn came, my answer to the fourth question was the same as the previous three: "Absolutely no idea whatsoever!"

To my relief the meeting eventually drew to a close. With most of the other reps already grappling with their allotted boxes and files, a now concerned Geoff shouted, "Paul, in your boxes are car stock samples, lipstick testers, various order books. All we've discussed over the past two days will give you plenty of food for thought over the weekend. Pay particular attention to all the literature. I look forward to seeing you again, bright and early on Monday morning, for your official induction into the company."

Shot away in all departments I began to trek my soaked trouser legs through dunes of snow on the first of what turned out to be more than a dozen tortuous return journeys to my snowbound car. Exhausted but determined to leave the scene as soon as possible I began to frantically scrape away the frozen ice from the windscreen, shortly to be overjoyed at my car key's triumph over the frozen lock. I bulldozed my way into my now miniaturised cockpit, kicked an obstinate box of lipstick testers clear of the gearstick, and screeched away Nigel Mansell style to the nearest pub, where I downed three large whiskies. If I were banned from driving, the only benefit would be that I would not have to relive this particular nightmare again for a few years!

My car enjoyed the entire weekend locked in my garage: all the boxes and sales materials remained completely untouched by human hand as I spent those two priceless days of freedom recovering from what was clearly the biggest bloomer of my entire crackpot working career.

Monday: 8.55 am. The venue: company head-quarters. The receptionist showed me to a large waiting room and explained that my sales manager would be with me shortly. A few minutes later I watched Geoff bounce along the corridor towards me, but the spring left his walk the moment he spotted me and it was in a flat, disillusioned voice that he said, "Good morning, Paul." The first part of my induction, he explained, would involve me watching the company video specially made for showing to all new employees. Ushering me into the Theodore suite dominated by a large video screen, he closed all the curtains and pushed a battle-scarred cassette into the video machine. Murmuring, "Enjoy the film. I'll see you later," he left the room. Seconds later, alone and isolated, I was knocked back in my chair by a loud blast of music, as appearing on the video screen in front of me was the panoramic view of the company's extensive American headquarters in Texas. The scene shifted to an opulent office interior containing vast expanses of marble. The camera now slowly zoomed in on the distant figure of F Henry Faxon III, eventually zooming in on his welcoming smile, the words 'Company President F Henry Faxon III' engraved in a plaque on his desk, and several large portraits of past company supremos hanging on the wall behind. He glared directly into the camera, topped by a halo of blue rinsed hair, looking as if, were he to be a jockey riding in the two o'clock at Newbury, he would be declaring at least fifteen stone overweight. He then took a deep breath, and with raised open arms said, "Welcome, new employee - not just to a new job but to our unique one-big-happy-family! Sit back in your chair, make yourself comfortable for the next two-and-three-quarter hours, and you'll be shown how this company started as a small shed in the back streets of Brooklyn and today has become one of the biggest cosmetics manufacturers in the world!" Moments later the first of a series of super-keen company executives was hard at work telling me how lucky I was.

I began to look anxiously at my watch, realising that I was to be imprisoned for at least another two and a half hours, and thought back to the start of my day some three hours earlier in the freedom of my local cafe. After ordering my usual two slices of toast and cup of coffee, I had begun my daily ritual of scrutinising each page of the racing papers for any bookmaker ricks. As my teeth were about to make first contact with my toast, an unwelcome blob of butter was already on its journey down to the left trouser leg of my only-been-worn-on-one-occasion suit. Frantic scrubbing at the resulting stain only managed to quadruple its size. Resigned to a dry cleaning job, I buried my nose deep into the pages of the Racing Post, only to be rocked by the sight of Coral's ultra-generous offer of 66/1 about Coventry's chances of lifting the FA Cup (the only possible explanation being that they thought the boys at Barking were now all on drugs) with 28/1 being the best offer elsewhere.

Excited as I was at the prospect of 'Getting On' and setting up a possible deluxe coup, a quick glance at the clock on the wall now showed 8.05 am. It suddenly dawned on me I actually had a job to go to.

Now, sitting here in solitary confinement - unable to get to a telephone, let alone a Coral's betting shop - I reflected bitterly that every self-respecting punting shark in the country would be 'On' except me!

With the machinery and conveyor belts on the screen slowly sending me into a state of hypnosis, I suddenly got the clue that proceedings were at last coming to an end when a close-up of the President once again appeared on the screen. Smiling like someone who had just bet 9/4 an 11/8 chance, and firmly clasping his hands, he looked directly into my eyes and then warmly said, "Welcome to your new family, and Good Luck!" As the figure of F Henry Faxon III slowly faded into the distance the show had at last drawn to a close. Moments after came the sudden loud 'click' of the auto cutout and the room was plunged into total blackness.

Although I knew I should go and look for Geoff, I decided that the brand of misery I was currently enduring might well be preferable to any of the further tortures which doubtless lay ahead, so I decided to stay put and continue my voluntary stretch of solitary confinement. About thirty minutes later I heard a gentle tap on the door and in walked Geoff. Blinded by the sudden light I raised my hands to shield my eyes. Struggling to my feet, I blurted out that the video had ended just seconds ago and how much I had thoroughly enjoyed it. Still squinting, and with both arms in mid air in front of me as if I were sleepwalking, I was then led away.

The afternoon started out better than expected, as I was honoured with the distinguished presence of the factory foreman who grudgingly escorted me on my standard induction tour of the factory. After that, though, things started to go downhill. Geoff, looking very assertive, led me away to his personal office where he began to battle his way through what can only be described as a jamboree paperwork spectacular, with additional product instruction manuals and never-seen-before order form explanations thrown in for good measure. My original intention, of absorbing as much information as I could, was abandoned within the first ten minutes, and I spent the rest of the time using what was left of my brain to make Geoff think I was listening to every word he was saying.

As the last piece of paperwork was transferred from Geoff's side of the desk to mine I realised that I had acquired enough new material to fill another half dozen boxes. Praying that another question time on the afternoon's activities was not about to follow, I was relieved when Geoff heaved a deep sigh and said that my official induction had now come to an end. However, I had further reason to worry as he reminded me that my P45, which he had expected to be handed in first thing that morning "as per my instructions given to you at Friday's meeting" was urgently required and I was told to "get the thing in the post to me tomorrow without fail." I could hardly explain to him that, because of my recent spell of unemployment, my P45 contained in the square which divulged my year's earnings to date the word 'NIL'. As he was under the impression that I had left my previous job the day before the sales conference, the consequences of letting him see it were unthinkable, and despite the inevitable screams from him that were sure to follow, I decided to proceed with my usual plan of sliding my P45 directly into the accounts office in about three weeks' time when it would be far less likely to be scrutinised!

As the obligatory handshakes and sounds of "Good Luck on your first day, Paul," faded, I was left with the chore of carrying my numerous newly acquired cardboard boxes to the car. Exhausted after completing yet another schlapathon, I drove straight to Coral's Ilford branch, praying that by some miracle I might still be able to grab some of that 66/1 Coventry.

As I flung myself through the shop door I realised that the last dog race of the day had just finished and John the bookie, already wearing his overcoat, was busy herding the last few stragglers out of the door. Always being one for a laugh and a joke, even in the most excruciating circumstances, and knowing full well that there was more chance of turning out for the Liverpool first team the following Saturday, I asked, "Any chance of betting a sixty six monkeys Coventry?" John, who was escorting Irish punter 'Harry the Hair' through the door, shouted back, "A few early skirmishers got on first thing this morning, but Coventry were 22/1 with us at just gone 10.30 am." I replied, "This job is costing me bundles already; the Ol' Bandit's completely shot away. I'll see you later."

The next morning, facing a very early breakfast and feeling rather depressed, I reflected that I had not been up this early since I had driven to the British Open the previous year: and that had been July, not freezing January. Turning the pages of my Sporting Life, only to be confronted yet again with the now best price of 22/1 Coventry, it once again registered in my brain that the repping job wasn't worth a carrot.

The company expected a minimum of ten calls a day, which meant spending an average of about forty minutes at each, so it was essential that I arrived at my first call in West Ham no later than 8.55 am. Inching my way down the Romford Road in the inevitable rush hour traffic, and surrounded by my fellow commuters, I realised that I had once again become part of the system I had previously always shunned. True, I had the blues but Tony Blackburn was enthusiastically at work trying to cheer all us happy workers up.

With the first signs of my therapy working, I was already considering the possibility of an early retirement and wondered whether it would be too early to make a claim on the company's pension scheme after just one week - but I had a feeling if anything I would be claiming on the health plan first!

One good result was not having Geoff with me because he was under the impression that the day's work was already second nature to me.

Forced to park a good half mile away, I headed for the store, with the weight of my briefcase causing me to waddle along the street like a lopsided penguin. Eventually, after struggling through the doors and then passing the largest collection of liquorice allsorts I had ever clapped eyes on, I approached the small, well-dressed, bald headed man busy chatting to a huddle of saleswomen. He reminded of a Sheffield-based bookie who had knocked me for fifteen hundred quid a few years back. Thinking that I must be looking every inch a sales rep and resting my briefcase on the floor, I waited patiently. Suddenly becoming aware of my presence and looking angry he bellowed, "Who are you with?" Midway through spluttering out my company name he barked back, "Well, you know what to do!" pointing to a small nearby door. I walked away, thinking that he must either be a close relation of that Sheffield bookie, or else countless hard-sell reps had conditioned him to be instantly obnoxious to all comers.

When I arrived at the dimly lit second floor

stockroom, the only sign of human life was a woman working way over in the opposite corner. A few words with her and I made my way back to where I'd first started from, realising that the dusty mountain of boxes I had passed contained my company's products.

Four and a half hours later, and still only halfway through my stock check, the sound of officious footsteps announced an unexpected appearance from the manager. "What the hell are you still doing here?" he snarled, adding, without stopping for a reply, "Freddie would have had the whole thing wrapped up in less than half an hour!" As he huffed off I thought, 'Cobblers to all this - I should be at the Wembley snooker anyway!' The new plan, I decided, was to quickly tidy up the boxes and crash straight in with my order book. These were almost identical to the multiple entry forms I used when trying to crack the 'Tote Jackpot', so to ensure a speedy job I imagined there was over two hundred grand in the Royal Ascot pool. Psyching myself up, I went down the card ticking off alternately six dozen and then nine dozen boxes of absolutely everything, knowing I'd crack the jackpot by getting out of this allergy-ridden dust-filled tip as quickly as possible. Last tick completed and order book already in my briefcase, I hurtled down the stairs two at a time.

After completing two laps of the track carrying the overweight penalty of my briefcase, and realising I was being checked by the manager, I proceeded to pull off the bluff of looking efficient. Eyes now scanning the stand from corner to corner while simultaneously adding at least a further fifty ticks to my already used jackpot form, I realised his small but menacing figure was marching towards me. Grim faced, he snapped, "I've just been upstairs! You've been here all this time and you haven't even done the damaged stock credits yet! Come with me!" Escorting me back to the stockroom he showed me a large cardboard box bearing the word 'Returns' and added, 'There it is.'

As the doors closed behind him I was already grappling with the box, which was on a shelf about a foot above my head. As I performed an exercise that only an Olympic gold-medal-winning weightlifter would have even considered, the force of gravity eventually took over, propelling the box through the latter stages of its journey towards the floor, where upon contact I found myself engulfed in a plume of glittering make-up particles, like a rainbow without rain. With hanky already over my mouth I flung myself into a corner to help save my lungs from further injury.

The dust subsided to leave a bumper jamboree mixture of eye-shadow kits, lipsticks and all manner of other cosmetic products I had not even realised existed. Even my limited knowledge of the game told me that Wonderful Freddie had not been doing his job as thoroughly as everyone had thought! The time was 4.00 pm, and with fatigue now well set in I was glaring at my stock credit return pad. Two hours later, and now reduced to my knees, I decided to make a guess at the rest and just get out as quickly as possible. Heading past the liquorice allsorts towards the doors, hoping could leave unnoticed, the manager shouted, "Next time you come bring your bloody tent!" As I marched out into the street, covered in a cocktail of Devil Red, Carnation Pink and Russian Resistance which threw the butter stain on my trousers into complete insignificance, I thought, "Don't worry mate, there won't be a next time!"

The next morning it took the full force of all three of my alarm bells to wake me from my coma.

I had already finished my toast and was starting on my third cup of Java in an attempt to bring myself round. My breakfast time ritual of scouring through the racing papers came to an abrupt halt when I spotted an article in the Racing Post pinpointing how it was possible to bet 11/4 an otherwise generally available 11/8 chance against Terry Griffiths winning that afternoon's Benson and Hedges snooker match. (It was also possible to bet the other player at 4/7, but paying the dreaded ten per cent betting tax made backing both players impractical - the Bandit's move would always be to bet the 'value odds' against playing a level stakes game.)

I had still not fully recovered from missing that 66/1 Coventry, and there was absolutely no chance the same mistake was going to be made today. The bookmakers concerned were a small multiple group based in the London area, but I also had access to them via a credit account or two.

A few seconds past the opening time of 9.30 am the telephones in their credit office were already ringing but after calling three individual 'monkey' bets, a grand total of just two hundred quid was actually accepted. At 10.20 am the manager of one of their local shops was busy refusing to take an £800 tax-paid bet from me, explaining that he had just spoken to head office and they would only accept £50. A quick sprint round three more of their shops resulted in my total stake for the day being £400, but it was all on at 11/4.

The first call of the day was to be a new superstore high street chemist, but with the time already being 11.35 am my chances of improving on yesterday's call rate were rapidly receding. Resting my aching arms for the few seconds it took my overweight suitcase to journey up the escalator towards the first floor, I proceeded to ask one of the young cashiers to direct me to the buying office. A few minutes later, and I was ushered into the presence of the branch's head cosmetics buyer, the very attractive Helen, thinking, 'I wouldn't mind being two lengths behind that, jumping the last fence at Ascot in a three mile chase!'

Helen immediately sensed that I would appreciate a little help from her to get me through the proceedings, and with a sexy smile told me to get out my order book. While I was fumbling through my briefcase she asked me what had happened to Freddie. "He suddenly got promoted," I replied, slowly, getting the odd clue that I might already be in with half a chance. Taking her order turned out to be a real 'no-aggro' experience, with my gaze alternating between her black fishnet stockings and my 'Tote Jackpot' order pad.

As I walked back out into the street I was now on an unexpected high with a value £400 snooker bet safely in the bin, my personal call rate record looking massive Odds On to be beaten, and Helen's phone number written on the back of one of the morning's betting slips for good measure!

Two small independently owned chemists' shops were next on the day's itinerary, but during the next three hours the owners, between them, managed to destroy my improving mental condition and leave me feeling like a white-haired raving maniac. The highlight was a mass ruck over my refusal to issue credit for what was described as 'over seven years without a rep getting round to list the damaged stock' from an owner who refused to accept my excuse that because I was a new rep I had not yet been issued with the pad I needed.

The next shop was a small chemist hidden away

in the back streets of Hackney, owned by one Mr Patel. As I walked through the door in a state not experienced since my four week spell a few years back with a plastics company (on that occasion, my doctor prescribed a short course of Valium to help me through my six days' notice!) I was greeted by one of my company's almost-empty display stands. Looking for the first signs of human life in a shop which looked as though it had been abandoned by its owner at least six months ago, I set about the task of checking the stock, which on this occasion consisted of three black mascaras and one Devil red lipstick. Five minutes later, with the shop still uninhabited, my initial whispers built up to a vibrating final yell that succeeded in producing Mr Patel.

As he shuffled towards me, sporting what could only be described as an unshaven rugged ethnic look, a closer examination revealed a mischievous expression complete with two prominent out-of-control roving eyes that made me think he looked more like an illegal betting shop bookie than a pharmacist.

I asked jokingly if he had been out the back watching the afternoon's snooker match on TV but he replied, snuffling through a bunged up nose, that he had been busy on the telephone. He led me round to the rear stock room, mumbling that business was very slow at present, together with instructions to order minimum quantities of only the very best-selling lines for him. The room itself was cluttered with countless toilet rolls, shampoo bottles and all manner of odds and sods, and looked like a junk yard. Standing at the nerve-centre of the Patel Pharmacy and with all clues screaming at me that he was definitely a fully-paid-up member of the skint merchants' club, I accepted the dubious honour of a seat on the battered - but definitely antique - official rep chair, and began to scratch out the order. As a past member of the very same club myself, I made sure that when he eventually received the invoice, he would get plenty of change out of a 'Bullseye'.

Mr Patel, clearly interested in my career change, then asked how I was doing in my new job. I told him, "I started seven days ago and already I'm a complete wreck! The whole thing is indescribable - major stress and strain and even my old chest pain problem has started up again, which for some reason usually coincides with acquiring any new job." Reflecting back to my days at the plastics company and with my eyes now wandering up and down rows of countless tablets, I asked if there was any chance of a Valium to calm me down. My request instantly sparked his shifty eyes into life and with a devious look now on his face he cunningly explained he could not supply certain drugs without a doctor's prescription.

Despite the rebuff I had a strong feeling that negotiations were not over just yet with the roguish Mr Patel when he hinted that Freddie used to 'look after' him. In an atmosphere full of expectancy, I decided to play my trump card and breathe the magic words 'Car Stock'. The response was instantaneous, his thoughts already fixed on the contents of the boot of my car. Clearly preparing himself to find out exactly how gullible I would prove to be against his subtle trickery, and with both eyes slowly scanning every corner of the room, he hissed, "What have you got?"

Sensing the imminent danger of being drawn into a haggling contest worthy of a Middle Eastern bazaar, and now very impatient to learn how my big value 11/4 bet on the afternoon's snooker match was progressing, I decided to make Mr Patel a giveaway deal he was unlikely to refuse.

Two minutes later I was poking about in the darkness of my boot: grabbing and stuffing my pockets with handfuls of anything that came my way I galloped back and unloaded the contraband on to his desk, and blurted out, "Mr Patel, you are now looking at over eighty pounds-worth of retail value, all I ask for in return is just one blue ten milligram Valium to help me survive through the rest of the day!"

Astounded by this unexpected avalanche of cosmetics and stunned into complete silence, it was at least thirty seconds before he was able to scramble over to the dispensary and begin his seemingly endless attempt to find just one individual tablet. Looking as though he'd just copped the Tricast in the Grand National, he returned to complete what must have been one of his best deals ever!

Mr Patel, already busy scooping his winnings into a large drawer, clearly now a friend for life, expressed how much he was looking forward to seeing me once again in six weeks' time. Leaving the bemused chemist behind, my thoughts were already switching to the current state of play in the snooker game. It was now 4 .15 pm and Mr Patel had been voted my last call of the day. Driving away to find a local cafe in which I would attempt to reorganise the confusion of my paperwork in time to catch the last post for Geoff, and desperately searching the airwaves for the latest sports update without success, I suddenly realised that I had just driven past a Dixons Superstore.

Now, while modern technology has on the whole done few favours for the super-shark punter in recent years, any angle enabling swift access to the latest sports information can be very useful, to say the least. I put my right foot firmly on the brake pedal, turned the steering wheel sharply and with a screech of tyres made an emergency U-turn, to the accompaniment of the crash of cosmetics sliding from starboard to port. I juddered to a halt directly outside the store, left the car with two tyres parked on the pavement, rushed through the doors and bolted over to the nearest salesman.

"Good afternoon," I said in my very poshest Colonel Devereux voice. I continued, "I'm considering purchasing a new colour television, but my wife has insisted it has to have that new teletext thing." Alert to a possible sale, he was eager to please. "Oh yes, sir, we have a number of models with tetetext, would you like a demonstration?" Replying, "I say, that's extremely nice of you," I followed him over to a rank of sets all tuned in to the same channel. "Have you ever used the teletext facility before?" he asked. "Unfortunately not," I replied. Picking up the control unit of a Deluxe twenty four inch Sony television, he opened proceedings by tracking down the latest weather forecast. Armed with the knowledge that heavy showers were on the way I enthused, "Amazing! I say, do you mind if I have a go?" "Not at all, sir," he replied. Now in full control and already tuned into the ITV channel, I proceeded to dial the familiar '130' number for the main sports index.

Instructed to dial page 143 for the 'Wembley Snooker latest' and with the salesman appearing bewildered, I eagerly stared as new combinations of numbers rolled into place like slot machine reels, to reveal that Griffiths was leading four frames to one. Over the moon and thinking that I was now only a short head away from a result the salesman, now thrown completely off whack, spluttered, "Well sir, as you can see it's great for sports coverage." Grabbing his right hand, I forced him into a lengthy handshake, chuntering on in my very best Devereux accent, "Thank you so much for your help. I'll discuss the affair with my wife this evening. Good day to you, sir!" while raising my imaginary top hat. As I marched upright towards the doors the salesman ran after me to retrieve the TV control unit which I was still firmly clutching in my hand: once outside I found that my car had the unwelcome addition of a parking ticket slapped on the windscreen.

A quick glance at my watch showed me that I had precisely fifteen minutes to complete Geoff's paperwork and catch the last post, but as I realised that it would take me at least five hours, I abandoned the cafe idea and decided to finish phase two of the day's ordeal at home, where I might have a chance of getting it ready for the first post in the morning.

Two hours later, the Bandit residence was looking like something out of Steptoe and Son, with grubby cardboard boxes and files scattered everywhere. My goal of grabbing a couple of hours' sleep was looking big odds against, as I was rapidly losing heart with the day's unfinished work. Feeling thoroughly depressed, I bent over the paperwork on my desk, taking the occasional glance at the television which was now permanently fixed on Oracle's page 143 confirming Griffiths' magnificent 5-2 victory - and which by now was providing the room with its only source of light.

The sombre silence was suddenly broken by two loud knocks at the front door. This did at least disturb the misery of my paperwork, and not really caring what kind of human life had come to visit me, I scrambled over a number of dusty cardboard boxes to be greeted by John. Looking his usual cheerful self, he explained that he was on the way to the 'Hurricane Higgins' match at Wembley and, his car engine ticking over, he wanted to know if I would like to come along.

Looking over my shoulder he exclaimed, "I thought you were a sales rep - I didn't realise you were in the storage business! No wonder you've been on the missing list recently!" Feeling sick and frustrated I replied, "It's called 'work therapy'.

I'm a non-runner tonight and the way things are looking I will be every night. It's going to take me ages to finish this bloody paperwork, but I'm so far gone I've decided to jib off tomorrow afternoon and fill my vacant place in the punters' club at Wembley." As John dashed off, I swallowed my ten milligrams of Valium to avoid possible suicide, and frantically scrutinised the pages of my diary for the first suitable departure date.

Fifteen days and I forget how many hours later, with the time at 8.05, am l drove north up the A12 to the small Essex coastal town of Burnham-on-Crouch towards a date with destiny. Due to the recent downturn in company business around the East London and Essex areas, Geoff had arranged to meet me, a few days earlier than originally planned, outside Cohen's Chemists at 9.00 am.

The quality of each working day had now reached an all-time low, but my immediate goal was to give Geoff the one week's notice needed to terminate this latest course of work therapy as soon as possible: this however would be easier said than done. To quote the words of the great F Henry Faxon III, "The only time one of our family members leaves is when they retire," but I was about to break ranks with the company's illustrious tradition! Fantasizing about the many permutations of how best to break this shock news to Geoff and how he would react, the very thought of working through my final week's notice launched a sudden feeling of pre-work charisma flowing once again through the Ol' Bandit's veins.

The pressure of my early morning assignment was no doubt responsible for my sweaty hands and the severe chest pains I was enduring as I approached Geoff's top-of-the range Cavalier which was already parked some twenty paces from Mr Cohen's Pharmacy. My preferred line of attack would have been to blurt out a no-nonsense, "Geoff, I'm afraid I've got a bit of bad news to tell you!" the moment I clapped eyes on him but as I opened the car door, fully pumped up and ready for the confrontation, events did not turn out quite as expected.

Geoff's minces had no doubt been well glued to his rear view mirror in anticipation of my arrival, and with the time already at 9.12 am were busy doing a little overtime. Before I could get started, he had sprung out of his seat, and smiling as though he had just gone through the card at Romford Dogs he dashed over to me and said, "Good morning Paul." Obviously, deciding to ignore the fact that I was a little late he went on, "I've been here for just under an hour preparing my monthly newsletter for the southern team, so perhaps you'd be kind enough to take care of Mr Cohen while I finish off?" In view of Geoff's good spirits I felt now was not the most opportune moment to give him the bad news. "No problem, Geoff," I replied, desperately trying to look as though I hadn't a care in the world.

Equipped with the briefcase, I was about to enter the business premises of Mr Cohen when Geoff shrieked, "I'd like us to get off to a flyer! I want to try and help you iron out some of the teething problems you're obviously having, so we've got a hell of a lot of work to cover!"

Barely visible over the top of the counter was Mr Cohen's head - bald, with the exception of a few silver-grey remnants of his former glory now neatly brylcreemed behind his ears. After the short chore of completing a stock check on his pre-war dispenser, the head eventually made its final journey out from behind the shop counter to finally reveal the complete torso of Mr Cohen. With the dubious pleasures of the rest of the day looming ahead of me, I was ready to be amenable to his every wish, and as he shuffled towards me I smiled and said brightly, "Good morning, Mr Cohen. How's business?"

With shoulders hunched, arms open and exposing the palms of his hands in a relaxed gesture he replied, "If I said business was good you'd think I was doing bad and if I said business was bad you'd think I was doing well." Obviously deciding to get down to real business, and looking a shade serious, he added, "Only order me minimum quantities of just a few of the best selling lines."

Realising he wanted to spend no more than a bar of soap, the order was completed in about two minutes, but with Mr Cohen insisting on personally scrutinising each individual item, no doubt to ensure he had not been stitched up, the in-depth discussion that followed delayed my departure by a further ten minutes. As I strolled back toward the car, about to enter round two but not yet able to deliver a knockout punch, Geoff's commitment to his paperwork appeared endless. His expression was clearly meant to deliver the message to all comers that he took the responsibilities of his job very seriously, but my return jolted him once again into overdrive as he shouted, "Paul, we'll use my car today. Take yours to the car park round the corner."

Three hours later, the interior of Geoff's car was beginning to feel like a mobile prison cell and I could not help but think my fellow inmate was teetering on the brink of insanity, having spent the previous hour explaining how his work load could not possibly be achieved in a normal working week and how he had devised a special work schedule for weekends and suggested I do likewise!

I was faced with a dilemma never experienced before in my work career. Geoff's frenzied enthusiasm was beginning to have a dire effect on my well practised routine for job resignations. Finding myself in the midst of round five of postponements, I was beginning to think that with a few more, the pools' panel would need to be summoned!

Our relentless schedule had taken us to Pinewood Pharmacy in Clacton-on-Sea where the stubborn owner, who at one time looked Odds On to order zilch, finally - after some forty minutes' hard sales tactics - succumbed to Geoff's cunning use of virtually every trick in the salesman's book and ordered well in excess of his usual stocks in addition to three dozen 'Deadly Nightshade' promotion packs! Bidding farewell to the bemused proprietor, Geoff, all beams and giving me a quick wink of assurance, dived into a nearby baker's, emerging with half a dozen cheese rolls which I gathered were to be our lunch. I lugged my briefcase back to the car, struggling to balance my allocation of rolls in my free hand.

Geoff, unable to remain silent for more than a few seconds, once again began singing the praises of the company's new world-beating promotion in between taking bites of his lunch, while I was nervously gulping mine in chunks. As we approached his car I realised my time had run out and our picnic would have to come to an abrupt conclusion. I dumped my briefcase next to Geoff's car, my cheese roll lunch a solid mass inside me, and prepared to meet my doom!

His head was buried deep in to the car boot in an attempt to locate his daily report pad which he proposed we should complete together, "this being one of your more serious weak spots!" Listening to his undecipherable mumblings I waited for him to re-emerge, feeling as if I'd just won the pools and forgotten to post the coupon! Realising I had arrived at the point of no return I took a deep breath and blurted, "I'm afraid I've got some bad news for you, Geoff." "What's that, Paul?" he asked with an air of grim expectancy. "Unfortunately I'm going to have to give the company one week's notice as from today for medical reasons!" The wheel had come off and Geoff, looking virtually paralysed, croaked, "What's the problem, Paul?"

Rubbing my rear nervously across the car wing

and in the process collecting yet more grime, I explained that about ten days ago, midway through an evening session of paperwork I suddenly experienced galloping chest pains and thought I was about to have a heart attack. I dashed down to the local casualty department and after three hours of tests was referred back to my local doctor. When I staggered into his surgery his first words were, "My God, sit down Paul, you look as though you're at Death's door!" and when I explained about the horrors of my new job he strongly advised me to consider leaving to avoid the future possibility of having to consult a psychiatrist friend of his.

Geoff stood there staring at me, mouth wide open and with a look of total bewilderment on his face, *a sight not witnessed since the '88 matchplay from the Mark McCumber punters who, already counting their winnings after being five up with seven to play, eventually found themselves part of a panicking stampede back to the public phones, jamming the bookies' switchboards in an attempt to 'bail out'.*

Geoff could only mutter, "I just don't understand!" - *ironically the very same words spluttered by one well known 'Face' who had been wiped out after Seve had crushed McCumber at the first play off hole.* Fidgeting with his tie and desperately trying to pull himself together, he continued, "This company over the past six months interviewed well in excess of five hundred candidates for this prestigious post, and we eventually entrusted it to you because you produced impeccable qualifications and interviewed exceptionally well. It's unbelievable that you've managed to survive less than three weeks!"

Looking imploringly up to the gods while shaking his head, his rage increasing by the second, he exploded, "I don't know what the hell has happened here but I must confess that from the word go the general standard of your work has concerned me! Freddie's area was the company flagship, but during your short stay with us it has nosedived to near catastrophe. Why you came to us in the first place is a complete mystery to me, but you are obviously not up to the job, and ultimately I'm the one who will be held responsible for your actions!"

The change in Geoff during the past few minutes had been so extreme as to remind me of the Incredible Hulk. He was almost bursting with rage and as he showered me with his splutterings I realised a quick left hook from his direction was not a big price. The backside of my already shot away suit polished the car wing as I slowly slid toward the muddy headlights with Geoff moving menacingly towards me, but then the clenched fist evaporated into a waving finger. Clearly incensed by my resignation speech and not relishing the impending task of phoning HQ to inform them that their new superstar had already 'cracked up,' he blurted, "You've survived with this bloody company less than three weeks!" Shaking with fury he blasted, "D'yer hear me ... less than three weeks and you're a goner, a failure, a f*!+?!g catastrophe!!"

As he scurried off to break the news to HQ, apparently in need of urgent psychiatric care, I felt relieved that the pleasures of my departure date were at last only one week away!

The windscreen wipers were only just winning their battle against the early morning deluge as my Cavalier travelled along the A12 on its final journey. The past few weeks had undoubtedly inflicted serious and possibly irreversible brain damage to the Bandit, but at long last I was shortly to be released from jail.

The previous evening I had ensured that all cardboard boxes, the briefcase, my leather-bound employee instruction manual - in fact, every item connected with the bloody job had now been stuffed into the car.

The contours of the Company HQ building eventually appeared through the rain and gloom, jolting me into the realisation that my current course of work therapy was at last approaching its conclusion. The same stone faced security guard I had encountered on previous visits demanded my security pass. I reluctantly wound down the car window. Glaring at short range with the peak of his cap directing trickles of water into the car, he remarked. "You look happy this morning."

"I am happy," I replied with a grin, "I'm leaving today."

My wing mirror gave me the final view of him still shaking his head disapprovingly as I slowly drove towards the front entrance. Reflecting on the misery I had endured throughout the previous few weeks, I despondently searched for a parking spot.

A good ten minutes later I was busy explaining to the receptionist that, sadly, I would today be leaving the company. Would she be kind enough to let Mr Hayden know I had arrived to finalise my departure? I found my one sided conversation being rebuffed by the once friendly Jane as she coldly interrupted to explain that Geoff had earlier left the message that he would be in conference all day and consequently would not be able to bid me an official farewell. My final salary cheque (which amounted to little more than a cup of tea) would be posted on to me within the next few days.

I had at the very least expected a few parting words from Geoff, but apparently even the predicted 'p*?s off and don't come back', would not be forthcoming. The final ceremony of 'the handing over of the company car keys' had on previous occasions been an emotional experience for all concerned, one way or another, but their release to the receptionist this time round was quick and completely painless.

The convenience of the company car and daily chore of modestly fiddling the expenses were pleasures that from today would exist only in my memory. Banished from the regiment and now stripped of all rank, the receptionist performed her duty of escorting me along the corridor towards the exit leaving me feeling like Chuck Connors in 'Branded'.

Empty wishes of good luck for the future were left fading into oblivion as I erected my collar in preparation for an assault on the prevailing monsoon conditions. The odds of a bus service operating through the centre of an industrial estate would be best compared to that of a named player achieving a 'nine dart check out' in the annual World Darts Championship. Having confirmed the estimated four mile hike to the nearest railway station, the security guard, together with the building that had for too long been the nerve centre of my ordeal, began to fade away into the distance, thank God forever. The torrential rain refused to give me any sort of a break as I reflected that on occasions retaining my place at the top of the order of merit on the crackpot punting tour sadly at times also involved enduring moments of intense pain.

I had always found it impossible to find any enthusiasm for a regular 9 - 5 job earning wages that would not even pay my betting tax. The punting game is one of the toughest, because no matter how many bookies are outsmarted or course records broken, unless you had preconditioned yourself to soak up pain suffered by the inevitable Double Bogeys and occasionally going out of bounds, the penalty to be paid is the one feared by all punters: 'Brain Damage'.

To deal with this, I developed a formula called work therapy which involved inflicting mental pain to myself for reasonably short periods of time by getting a proper job. When the job suddenly stopped this would result in me being instantly catapulted to punting success. My most recent spell of treatment - a shade more intense than usual - would no doubt hold me in good stead as I prepared yet again for battle with the country's already beleaguered bookmakers.

4. ON THE ROAD

Rubbing away incessant cigar smoke from my eyes, like Alice returning from Wonderland, I found myself re-united with the Magnum Moustache who was toasting my good health, apparently now convinced I was Bjorn Borg! I was only too pleased to provide my autograph, as he assured me my moniker would guarantee his prompt departure.

The sight of late evening company p*?s ups only increased my determination to successfully land our biggest coup to date, because if it wasn't made to happen I would probably end up being part of yet another great big happy family.

<u>12.15 pm, Nottingham the next morning</u>.

"Well, it's just an idea I got from a golf magazine that did an article about hole-in-one's," John explained, to a bookmaker who only moments before had revealed he was the local golf team captain and would quote no bigger than 1/3.

The annual early spring precipitation appeared to be way above average as John trudged back to the car, still feeling slightly apprehensive. Yesterday's Arthur Whittaker shock waves could well have spread in the prevailing easterly direction, but the vibes so far had proved to be reasonably encouraging, with no 6/4 quotes, 3 'not interested', 2 'don't know' and 1 'get lost', reading rather like an opinion poll.

With the ritual of recording the 1/3 quote completed, within minutes we were travelling through the back streets of Nottingham towards the betting premises of Coleman Commissions.

Much twisting of necks and a NASA style street number countdown eventually led John into a converted terraced property. Following a quick round of patter that clearly went in one ear and out the other, the disinterested manager, at a guess in his late fifties, shuffled off to the back room to drag out 'Gaffer'.

The bespectacled Coleman seemed to be a regular sort of guy as he patiently listened to the inevitable rerun. "Hmm, a hole-in-one," he mumbled, looking a shade puzzled. "A draw on a boxing match is about a 50/1 shot - I'll lay you the same," he then decisively said.

Trained to retain his composure, John presented him with a Hole-in-One request for St. Mellion and rather timidly asked how much he could have on. "Anything you like," he boldly replied.

A judgement would now have to be made. How much stake money does John attempt to invest without the risk of blowing himself out, because the last bookie who had made an identical offer had virtually collapsed at the sight of a tenner?

The anxious passing over of the fifty pound note went without visible emotion as efficient Coleman briskly completed the formalities and presented John with his carbon copy. The bet had been accepted so sweetly that despite the friendly good-byes that had taken place, John just had to find an excuse to crash in again.

A brief study of the Jackson and Lowe Lincoln Handicap Ante Post special sellotaped to the wall provided him with what turned out to be the all important clue. Beaumont Girl 50/1, clear favourite to be a non runner, and therefore the perfect nag to bet on.

"I might as well have a bet on the Lincoln before I shoot off - can I take the 50/1?" John, casually asked presenting his £50 to win Beaumont Girl betting slip. "No problem," replied the bookie with renewed interest.

"By the way, can I have another £50 on the hole in one bet?" asked John, praying to the gods for the answer to be yes. "Sure," replied the bookie with a confident nod. As fast as a Vegas Blackjack dealer, John produced Hole in One bet number two together with yet another nifty, which was gratefully accepted as Coleman wished him the best of luck. "I'll need it if it's pouring down like this at the golf," John shouted back, beginning his unwelcome dash to the car.

The five thousand pounds to a bar of soap celebrations were short lived, as the other face could be seen venturing into the rain earnestly looking in all directions.

John dived beneath the dashboard and began an intense study of the complex wiring around the car radio area, because this probably meant that either Coleman had received a quick '6/4, mate' from Coral's, or maybe he was just wondering where the guy with a London accent had disappeared to after leaving behind that unexpected £165 donation.

Compelled to immediately withdraw from the area, it took us a good hour and a half to drive to the next targeted bookie, this time using the Leicester itinerary. Tremendously uplifted at having the day's target already in the bin, the 'not interested' straight treble that followed was reasonably easy to take on the chin.

The local bookies listed in the Leicester Yellow Pages served to prewarn us that the Shamrock Racing Betting Shop we were approaching had only one chance in eight of being the company's sought after base branch, and it was to be the Bandit who would investigate ...

Minutes later the negative vibes I received from the guy behind the counter told me that on this occasion I had probably not backed a winner. I had two options - the first being to ask the manager if the owner could be located at one of the other branches, and the second being simply to ask what price the Shamrock Racing outfit offered for a Hole-in-One in a golf tournament, and simply hope for the best. I decided to take my chances with the latter.

"I'll give the Governor a quick ring," he agreeably told me as he leapt to his feet to acknowledge my most unusual request. The short conversation, to my relief, ended with him still retaining his inquisitive smile.

"The guv'nor says he'll lay 7/4 any golf tournament," he informed me in a manner that suggested only a man possessed would even consider suggesting such a proposition. "Is it possible to bet a fivefold accumulator?" I calmly asked.

"I can't see a problem, but I'll have to give him a tinkle back to make sure," came the startled reply.

7/4 odds when 50/1 had been obtained earlier in the day may not, on first analysis, appeal: but this was clearly a very substantial business with a £50,000 winnings limit displayed. With - in our judgement - each of the five bankers representing Even Money chances at best, the opportunity to place a decent bet on the lot copping, and still probably to get paid out was simply too good to miss.

The short exchange of mumblings followed by his reassuring nod was the green light to scratch out the five banker events and attempt to bet them in a 'The lot must cop to collect' 156/1 accumulator.

"My interest for the year," I enthused, plonking my £220 Hole-in-One special on the counter. I was earnestly funking he would just ring my bet through the till without fuss, enabling me to quickly bin the slip and shoot off, but a glimpse at my readies activated his hand to clench the phone, intending presumably to seek authorisation from the big boss man himself.

The sudden unwelcome return of my galloping chest pain problem forced me to take a seat for the few moments it took him to make the call, but the blurred vision of him ringing my bet through the till without a steward's enquiry caused me even greater concern.

The manager's boat came back into focus with the fanning then the presentation of my eagerly awaited slip. "See you in September," he jokingly shouted as I finally made my way to the door. The 156/1 accumulator odds made it look as though I was disappearing into the early evening dusk forever, but with the bet in our view being no more than a 10/1 chance to cop, a return was far more probable than he envisaged.

It was John's chance to have a crack with his own brand of lingo the next morning. When he hadn't returned after about twenty five minutes of entering the fifth betting shop of the day I hoped he was making full use of his golf tournament fixture list, but unfortunately he was in a state of much distress.

"No ... no ... don't drive yourself mad," begged John, attempting to halt telephone enquiry number eight.

"It's only a crackpot idea, forget it, I don't even want the bloody bet," John continued in desperation, fearing the unwelcome 'nause' was causing Hole-in-One havoc throughout the area.

"It's no trouble at all, lad," insisted the bookie as

the phone rang at Stanley Racing.

"You only offer Evens - are you sure?" John heard him say as he replaced the receiver, appearing totally baffled. Saving himself from further telecom donations, the bookie thankfully accepted John's final 'forget about it' as, relieved, he eventually made his way to the car.

The Ol' Bandit's success expectations were soon demolished as John blurted out his unfortunate tale. "He must have gone through the card with the locals then started on the multiples - I tried everything to stop him," he grimly explained.

I calmed down a bit as we made our way to the next call, 'Patterson's Turf Accountants', now praying they had not been prewarned of our imminent visit. John walked in casually: a bright yellow cardigan appeared tailor made to accompany the strong presence of a middle aged character complete with Bobby Charlton haircut. Glued to the shop's only SIS screen, he was vigorously condemning to all present the previous day's disgraceful decision by the stewards to disqualify poor Willie Carson for 7 days.

The 'Dwell up Stakes' was a bit of a nuisance, but John made himself at home by gazing yet again at the sports betting pages of the Racing Post, giving Yellow Cardigan a good five minutes to settle down inside the shop's control module before cagily making the first move.

The unwelcome Russian Roulette game of 'Did

the last Bookie phone the next Bookie' always played havoc with John's nerves, but with there being little value in mucking about, the 'offence' was ready for action. The "Hello mate, I'm going to the golf in a few days time," intro revealed on this occasion John had fortunately drawn a blank as Bob Patterson stuffed his hands in the pockets of his cardigan and listened attentively.

"It's short odds you know," he casually said after a few moments' deliberation on John's request. "The last time we laid that bet we quoted 7/1", he then continued, biting a chunk out of his fruit and nut bar.

"I only want a small bet for an interest," explained John in reply, prompting a positive response.

"You can have that if you want a bet, son, but only for small money - ten or twenty quid," he said, spurring John's unconcerned withdrawal to the 'Patterson's' betting slips.

The intended bets consisted of ten tenner doubles (full cover re the five bankers) but getting the lot on would be anything but easy. "I'll be going to most of the big golf tournaments during the year," John said, tentatively.

"Is it possible to have a few doubles for peanut stakes to give me a small interest in each event?" he then anxiously asked, preparing for the moment of truth. "No problem, so long as you don't bet the same double twice," came the reply.

Despite having all ten doubles at the ready, it would be a foolish move to suddenly present him with the lot like Paul Daniels, because this would only increase the danger of him suddenly changing his mind. John decided instead to buy a couple of minutes by breezing through the 'Pattersons' fixed odds football coupon before returning with just five of the slips.

The quite substantial liability he would incur with each double clearly was not registering in his brain as he nonchalantly scratched out the 7/1 odds with his red pen next to each event and briskly fed them through the shop till. "Can I scratch out a couple more before I shoot off?" John asked, as an approving nod propelled him to the nearest betting slip to make preparations for an attempted 'Late Entry'.

The remaining five doubles were being pulled from John's trouser pocket well inside the two minute barrier as Bob promptly completed Hole-in-One acceptance procedure phase two. "A super Yankee is five selections?" John enquired as the readies-for-carbon-copies exchange was being made.

"I may as well have this, just in case by some miracle the lot cops," John continued, following Bob's predicted reply. The red pen thankfully was at work within seconds as the £8.78 potential kiss of death (30p super yankee all five bankers) received Bob's prompt attention.

"Sorry I was so long, but it was worth it," said

John to the Bandit, returning to the co-pilot's seat in the car. "He only wanted to take a couple of twenty quid bets at 7/1, but by the time I'd finished it's now bang on the cards we'll take him for the £20,000 shop limit."

Inside Betting Shop No.12 ... and all was not going well for John.

"Right, where is he?" came the thunder from the back office only moments after he had handed the completed St. Mellion Hole-in-One slip to an elderly, rather frail looking gentleman, just hoping for the best. Exploding into the shop area, the manager looked a bit like a Sumo wrestler ferociously waving the slip above his head, barely in control. "You've been all over the place with this bet," he said angrily. John prepared to pay the price for that bloody nause's earlier telethon.

"What's it all about mate?" he bravely asked: being on the wrong end of a 'Boston Crab' within the next few seconds was no bigger than the chance of six to four On. "Do you want me to call the police?" he then surprisingly blurted as John resolutely held his ground.

"Is there some crime in asking a bookmaker to quote odds - I thought that's what this game was all about?" John asked him defiantly.

"I know your game," he blurted back in retaliation. "You're not having me over so p*?s off," he continued, pointing a finger towards the exit door.

"If Tesco's are selling a tin of baked beans for 47p and another supermarket charges 52p, I'd probably buy from Tesco's. All I'm doing is shopping around for the best deal I can get," John nervously argued, deciding that now would be a convenient moment to proceed with his departure.

The following morning...

"Hello Ted, I've got him in the shop now - the hole-in-one man." These words, sarcastically blurted down the phone from one so called fearless bookie to another at that final stumer call yesterday evening, were still ringing in John's ears, and with his nerves still on the blink and in desperate need of a 'Patel' valium tablet, we decided it was time for me to change from my role as mundane cab driver into the greatest real life power on earth - Bandit Power.

St. Mellion was now only three days away and as we approached Rubble Racing, time was becoming an even bigger enemy than the bookies themselves, so I was even more determined than ever to give the day one hundred and ten percent.

The expensive Rubble Racing fascia made me think this was probably a branch belonging to a larger Group, but John, already re-checking the itinerary sheets for both Derby and Leicester, assured me this was still a good Odds On chance to be an independent bookmaker. Wearing the famous stars and stripes colours selected from my extensive rugby shirt wardrobe, it took me a good five minutes to psych myself into a new personality change, ready to bring to life one of my favourite characters - notorious cockney splodger Del Duffer.

Approaching the shop window, I took a few moments to ponder at the impressive line up of action sporting superstars. The magnificent swing of Seve Ballesteros was left behind as I found myself standing on a plush red carpet garnished with horse head motifs.

The interior had been fitted out to a standard any multiple company would have been proud of, with the modern technology of twelve SIS screens providing entertainment for the inevitable sprinkling of early morning codgers. The enthusiasm of the presenter appearing on screen No.1 was hard to believe as he eagerly explained that there would be additional live coverage from Ireland's NAAS Racecourse until 6.25 pm together with the final four races from the Canterbury dog card.

The Rubble Racing caption proudly displayed on each screen was taking full advantage of the odds-compiling skills of Graham Sharpe and the rest of the William Hill team with early prices for the day's principal races, updated sporting events and two screens reserved exclusively for the St. Mellion Golf.

The guy seated at mission control was hard at work probably knocking out the night dog bets, but wearing a smart pinstripe suit, white shirt and gold rimmed glasses, he looked more suited to the role of bank manager than bookie. It didn't look as though he would suffer fools lightly, but all the clues pointed to there being a reasonable chance he would lay a lumpy bet - so there being little point in mucking about, the Ol' Bandit decided to make his move.

"Hello Guv'nor, I can have as much on at these odds as I want, can't I?" I bellowed, shaking the shop into life. "There's no sweat in betting an eighteen thousand to two Faldo, is there?" I continued, marching towards the counter already counting a fistful of readies.

Catapulted to his feet and looking a shade confused, the softly spoken bookie bravely told me I could bet what I liked, providing the odds were quoted on the shop screens. "There's a few things I want to bet on," I bulldozed on, completing count two of my readies and adding that I had ironed out 'three large' at the dogs the previous evening.

"I want to bet Mike (Harwood) to beat Brand Jnr in the matches and while I'm here I'll lay out a few quid on the cricket," I enthusiastically continued, pointing up to the screens. "Where's the 2,000 guineas betting - I want a price for Desert Sun," I then shouted, pacing the floor.

"Just give me a second," came the accommodating reply as he pressed into the SIS computer for the latest William Hill odds. "The latest price is - 10/1, Sir," he politely informed me, insisting I take a pipe at his monitor.

"Missed the f*!+?!g train again," came my disgruntled reply as I threw my arms up in frustration. "There's no hole-in-one odds up on the screen - can you quote me a price, guv?" I then briskly enquired.

His face, thank God, only produced a mild frown as he once again sought refuge with the William Hill golf pages on his monitor. Shaking his head and mumbling hole-in-one to himself, he soon predictably blurted, "There's nothing about hole-in-one's on here - give me a few minutes and I'll sort something out."

As I prepared to endure the dreaded phone around, I decided to take a pitch directly in front of the army of SIS screens, and began scratching out my bets using the palm of my hand as a rest - fully aware that from under his glasses the bookie was discreetly clocking the Ol' Bandit's every move.

With no visible looks of horror so far the recorded vibes were reasonably good, so when he put the phone down and began scratching his head after the third call, I felt a quick word was in order. "How'd you make out, Guv?" I blurted, ready to offer assistance.

"What price did you get last year?" he asked desperately in search of a clue. "66/1," I truthfully replied, staring him straight in the eye. "You can bet that, then," he told me, casually shrugging his shoulders.

He clearly thought there was more chance of Martians landing in the shop within the next three seconds than the 'bet' copping at St. Mellion, but despite a strange shiver of expectancy running through my veins I had to be sure he was convinced he had one deluxe mug splodger in the shop before making my Hole-in-One move.

"I want to bet fifteen hundred quid like to beat Brand Jnr in the match and I'll pay on Guv," I positively told him.

Grabbing his pen, he made his way back to the SIS computer keyboard and was shortly running his finger down the monitor until reaching the 11/10 Harwood. "You can't take the p*?s out of me Guv so I do me dough with the tie," I continued earnestly, counting my readies.

(Some Bookmakers offering match bets include the tie - If scores are level after four rounds, stakes placed on either golfer would be lost.)

After a few moments thought he said, "If you want Tie No Bet, the best I can lay you is Evens." "That'll do, guv, and I'll pay the tax," I replied, eagerly handing him a wad of fifties. He appeared apprehensive as he began wading through the readies, occasionally peering over his glasses and only too aware that there were more bets to follow. Towards the end of the count and impatiently on the buzz, I interrupted. "This hole-in-one bet - I don't want to do my b!?*?+ks on that, but let me have a two'er at 66."

He gave me a wily smile from under his glasses in reply, so I wasted little time in pushing the £220 together with slip towards the Harwood count, steadfastly continuing despite dropping down a gear.

"I want to bet an eleven hundred to ten the draw in the cricket." My passionate outburst was continued with the grand from my rear pocket being slapped on top of the bet. "I've got to have an interest in the test, guv, it's live on Sky One at 9," I earnestly told him, retaining one hand on my grand.

His eyes momentarily alternated between the further cash injection under my hand and the Hole-in-One slip, but he was soon busy binning the £220 stake money and scratching out the 66/1 odds with a red pen. "That's 11/10 and I'll pay the ajax," I blurted, sliding my grand towards him while feverishly pointing at the test odds on screen 8 - but seemingly unperturbed, he methodically completed the transactions.

"It's funny guv, I didn't even know you were here, otherwise I would have played the game with you in the past," I blurted, peeling off the tax money from my inside pocket supply of readies.

"I've got a few big players," he responded promptly, passing me the annual Rubble Racing diary and business card. "I offer my regulars the best prices where I can - I'm in business to keep them happy," he continued, keen to recruit a new mug.

"I don't care about betting under the odds, you

can even lay Ladbrokes prices if you lay me a half decent bet," I resolutely told him, briskly making my way to the door.

The Ol' Bandit now had to take immediate action - to cancel those unwanted cricket and match bets.

Once again passing the Seve swing, I promptly made my way back to the car phone. "Good morning, can you confirm Gordon Brand Jnr is Evens to beat Harwood in your St Mellion golf betting," I asked the accommodating female voice on the Victor line." "Yes, he is, sir," came her immediate reply.

The reputable Victor Chandler firm had advertised golf match odds (Tie No Bet) in the Life, and knowing they were not afraid to lay a decent bet, I asked for fifteen hundred quid at Evens 'Guess who'.

Seconds later ... "Thank you Sir, I'll read that back. You have fifteen hundred pounds at Evens, Gordon Brand Jnr. to beat Mike Harwood, tax paid."

The task of phoning around for the test cricket shows had earlier been completed by John so my fingers already knew which digits to press next on my car phone. "Can you give me a show on the test match, please," I enquired in all innocence, "Who do you want to bet?" came the abrupt reply.
"To be honest I haven't decided yet," I told him, sensing the call had to be handled with care.

"It's 6/1 Australia, 6/4 The Draw and 7/4 the West Indies," he then informed me. "Umm, I'll have eight hundred quid on the West Indies if that's OK," I modestly requested, realising there was more chance of me shooting a 59 round Wentworth next Sunday than this lot taking a 'TH'.

"Just a minute, Sir," came the predictable response. The indiscreet mumblings lasted about the usual three or four minutes before he reluctantly made his return. "Sir, I've just had a word with the racing manager and he will only authorise four hundred pounds at 7/4," he pathetically informed me.

"Fine, I'll take it," I told him, realising it would be futile to do anything else, but relieved they hadn't pulled their standard, 'It's just a fun bet so we're only taking ponies, Sir,' stroke.

Just moments later John had no problem betting a six hundred to Four with one of his prized accounts, and following my no aggro hundred quid on Australia at a top of the shop 20/1, the telephone splodge was concluded.

"What's it all mean?" asked a confused John, as I completed some mental arithmetic. "The match bets have ironed out three hundred quid whatever happens," I despondently told him.

"The test wins a tenner," I continued, and Rubble Racing have laid us over thirteen thousand pounds to two hundred quid the St. Mellion hole-in-one," I enthused, as we found ourselves propelled yet one more step up the success ladder towards the ultimate goal.

The good run continued as the day produced two Monster Hole-in-One time devices being planted in the East Midlands' area, set as usual to explode at intermittent golf events. With St. Mellion now just days away, the long but highly effective spring campaign was drawing to a conclusion with to-morrow (Tuesday) reserved exclusively for 'call backs'.

"Woosie's just won the Masters so he'll probably be knackered - Olazabal will need time to recover from his blow out - Faldo's shot away right now anyway. I fancy Langer, he loves the course and I remember last year he was eight over par after the first two holes but still finished third in the tournament." I discussed with John as we started on the morning's third cup of coffee at Motorway Services somewhere on the M1.

We had been reading through the pages of the Life and Post in turn, but our unanimous conclusion after careful scrutiny of the match and group betting on this occasion was - Don't think about having a bet until the tournament is underway. Hitting the road, we felt any business done would be a bonus. By lunchtime, after quite a hectic morning session, the blank spaces beside each target's name on the itinerary sheets were beginning to disappear.

I recalled the abrupt manner in which that burly middle aged bookie had told me to "Call back another day, can't you see I'm busy?", in reply to my brief Hole-in-One enquiry, foolishly blurted out bang in the middle of an afternoon's racing. I could so easily have blown myself out forever, but here I was again, given a second chance as I made my way into the licensed betting premises belonging to 'Bentons T/A' this time about half an hour before the first race.

I had a good clue that this guy wasn't skint, because a build up of 50 pence forecast merchants queuing at the counter had for a good few minutes remained unattended. It was difficult to understand why he hadn't spent a few quid improving the decor but when he appeared through the rear door blurting, "You can't beat a good crap," I realised he had little ambition to improve the class of his regular clientele.

I remained schtum until he got round to sellotaping the day's Sporting Life results sheet to the top of a pile of old issues. Using the varying shades of yellow as a clue, they must have dated back to the 'Pinza' Derby year.

"Whey Hey," I blurted, disrupting the daily ritual. "what price did you manage to sort out for me?" I optimistically continued, realising if it was only 'Each of Two' my previous enquiry would already be erased from his memory.

"You wanted a price for a hole-in-one, if I remember rightly," he cautiously replied, scratching his head.

An unwelcome interruption came from an elderly 'Hooter' telling the bookie, "There's quite a lot of those you know - some Yank got one in the Open at St. Andrews only last year." The stress and strain of this game over the years has played havoc with my nerves. I've never been one to complain, but please - give me a break.

"Have you ever had a bet on this before?" he then cagily asked with the 'Hooter' still at hand. "All I can say is last year I had a few bets at 40/1 with a Birmingham bookmaker and the year before that the biggest independent bookmaking group in London, 'Mannings', laid me 10/1 for the British Open," I began to explain, pulling the disintegrating but bona fide betting slip out of my rear pocket for inspection, "and 'Coral's, one of the country's leading multiples, were quoting 16/1 for the same event," I continued, using all the weaponry at my disposal to best effect.

"I wouldn't mind a bet at those odds myself, Ted," interrupted the 'Hooter' once again.

"One of the big bookies are bound to have some odds," Ted then told me, already running a finger down countless miniaturised phone numbers on a betting slip sellotaped to the wall.

"There's no point in bothering with all that," I assertively told him raising my voice. "I've already asked most of the big bookies but for some reason they are not quoting odds for this event - that's why I'm asking you."
"I'll try Demmy's - they quote odds for everything," he blurted back to my dismay.

The jovial enquiry to the trade room soon entered into deep discussion with occasional nods from Ted agreeing with whatever words of wisdom were being transmitted from the Demmy Command Centre.

When he eventually slammed the receiver down appearing somewhat displeased I had a fair idea what was coming next. "Who laid 40/1," he angrily asked.

"I told you, it was a Birmingham Bookie - I think the name was Peter (Midlands)," I replied, on the defensive.

"Bet he's skint now," he fired back. "Demmy only go Evens," he went on, pointing to the phone. "They told me all the Northern Bookies have been bombarded with this bloody bet - nothing to do with you, of course?" he then sarcastically suggested, clearly taking the misguided view that I had intended to embark on some form of dastardly stitch-up.

The angry cold stare and one open mouthed 'Hooter' were my only goodbyes as I began the long walk to the door. "I can't believe these merchants," I told John as I fumbled to push my keys into the ignition.

"They're happy when the place is mobbed out with punters ironing out readies on computer forecasts and multiple bets at S.P. all day, but when someone walks in to try and gain an edge at the game, fair and square, you'd think an horrendous offence was being committed," I went on as we began what turned out to be an exasperating two hour slog round five branches belonging to the

Sports Investment Group in search of the elusive owner, but when we eventually found ourselves gazing at that sparkling red BMW taking pride of place parked across the shop frontage we thought all our troubles were over.

I didn't fancy my chances too strongly here, because the branch managers would probably between them already have set off the alarm bells, but the manner in which the four way jovial clowning behind the shop counter came to a conspicuous halt within seconds of my arrival suggested that from the word go I would have to be on my toes.

The young guy with the prominent blond highlighted hair and well used leather jacket was rank outsider of the four to be the bookie, but when he took the initiative and arrogantly told me, "I'm laying 3/1 if you want a bet," it was enough to put you off 'Jollys' for the rest of your life.

"Whey Hey," I blurted back, forcing a smile, "I've been having a quick pipe round the other branches trying to get hold of you," I feverishly continued, realising he knew as much anyway.

He thought quoting 3/1 was another way of telling me to get lost but when I asked if it were possible to bet doubles and trebles he was only too ready to call my bluff. "You can bet 3/1 till the cows come home," came the brash reply, prompting me to take a seat at the only table.

The cocky bravado, together with a £25,000 shop limit, invited an immediate attack, so I began to make repetitive but essential preparations. The game of 'Poker' began as I threw a monkey and my first hand of betting slips into the pot.

He made his move and methodically began to accept the doubles with only the sound of the shop till breaking the uncomfortable silence.

The 'Trebles' play produced movement in the old bottleometer stakes, with a noticeable decrease in the pace of his pen, but as each bet found its way through the till, my hand was rapidly improving. The Ol' Bandit knew the kid never had a chance with the deck stacked massively against him.

Raising the stakes, I decided to play my ace card. "A tenner super Yankee OK?" I casually asked, realising the shop limit would be obliterated if the lot were to cop but very much looking forward to expressing my displeasure at the presentation of my £25,000 winners cheque.

"I'll take it, but that's your lot," he blasted, snatching the slip and finally throwing in his hand.

The late call was just what we needed to officially end phase one of the campaign on a high note, having created a potential bumper payday of £1/4 million. We drove back to our base camp, praying that the gamble of investing many thousands of pounds in stake money and expenses, together with weeks of relentless hard work, would be rewarded ... but we still needed one thing to make it all worthwhile - LUCK.

Our minds were set on cruise control for most of

the three hundred mile drive down to Cornwall the next day, but when I decided to tune the radio into a local FM station about ten miles from Plymouth and heard the chirpy weathergirl announce "North Easterly winds with heavy showers will continue to keep temperatures well below average for the time of year," the ominous thought of a golfer standing on a Par 3 tee freezing his cobblers off together with icy winds blowing the balls off target were none too inspiring.

Prior to 1990 the prestigious Benson and Hedges event had for many years been held at Fulford (near York), but as we briefly reminisced about the previous year's ultra-early Andrew Sherborne 'ace,' the familiar outline of the Holland Inn, Saltash, reappeared.

"The weather's been humpy all month, Sir - it's a pity they decided to hold the tournament so early this year," the barman explained, acknowledging our recollection of the glorious conditions at the previous year's event.

Two pints of the local brew had encouraged the conversation to move onto Bookmaker disreputability - a subject very close to the Bandit's heart - and how the muggers in the game had never ceased to amaze him.

"What about TNS bookmakers?" he passionately went on to recall.

"I was absolutely over the moon when Higgins won that snooker event. I was the proud owner of a TNS voucher confirming my six hundred quid each way at

12/1 apart from a bull's eye each way for a mate, but when I read the Life's investigative report questioning the financial stability of the TNS Empire one morning, the cornflakes went spinning."

Punters alarm over bookmaking firm

By BRIAN RADFORD

PRESSURE is mounting heavily on bookmakers TNS. Anxious punters and bookmakers kept ringing The Sporting Life yesterday demanding to know whether the Cheltenham company was still in business.

One angry punter said that he was owed £7,000 and that a cheque for £2,000 of this sum had bounced this week.

Another Yorkshire punter was owed £5,000 and his cheque had bounced three times.

To open an account with TNS, all clients are requested to place a deposit. In some cases it can amount to £8,000.

Clients are now worried that even these may not be returned.

Terry Higgs became managing director of TNS in April 1978. His co-director was Peter Glanville, a bookmaker. Both men secured 26 shares and began with a nominal capital of £1,000.

Glanville resigned three years ago and "gave" his shares to Higgs.

Further problems developed yesterday when a large firm of bookmakers took legal advice concerning Higgs personally over an unpaid gambling debt of more than £90,000.

They said cheques from Higgs had bounced three times. Two other multiple companies are also trying to obtain money from him.

TNS have 500 clients and, in addition to these telephone accounts, they own two betting offices in Cheltenham.

Higgs is known to be a keen gambler and one company said it was not unusual for him to bet up to £30,000 a day.

One bitter punter, Liyuen Fong, a Mauritian from Balham in London, said: "TNS owe me about £7,000, including £2,000 which they are holding as a deposit.

"They sent me a cheque for £2,000 today and it bounced. When I rang them a person said the business was being sold and that I would have to speak to the people who took over."

A professional punter from York said his £5,000 cheque had bounced three times. He also had £800 in a deposit account.

He said: "I rang them today and lost my temper. What annoys me is that they are still taking bets.

"I'm a fair chap. I work my horses out on form. I'm not one of those knockout people."

Another credit punter from Cornwall said that when his £300 did not arrive yesterday, TNS told him their bank had advised not to write further cheques until the business was sold. This punter had a deposit account of £60.

A Scottish client with £200 tied up in a deposit came home from work to a bouncing cheque of £300.

He said: "It wouldn't be so bad, but I was £2,000 down to them just two weeks ago."

Yet, despite their massive problems, TNS still advertise in this week's Raceform Handicap Book that special tax concessions (tax free up to 30 minutes before first race) are available and boast of a £250,000 win limit.

Besides his position as director of TNS, the redoubtable Higgs has worked as an accountant for the American-owned Prestolite who manufacture motors for fork-lift trucks. He resigned on November 9.

A spokesman said: "Mr Higgs had been with us about seven years."

Higgs was not available for comment last night. A supervisor at Cheltenham Telephone Exchange said Higgs had asked for an ex-directory number on Wednesday and specifically requested "no calls".

The Ol' Bandit's entire fortune at that time had been entrusted into the safe hands of one Mr. Higgs, but realising a quick withdrawal was an absolute must, dashed to the car and headed for the HQ in Cheltenham.

DEPOSIT ACCOUNTS: THE LEGAL POSITION

FOLLOWING the collapse of TNS. who specialised in deposit accounts. The Sporting Life has been asked a variety of questions concerning the legal position. Here are some of the questions and a lawyer's advice:

Q—If one opens a deposit account with a bookmaker and the bookmaker cannot settle winning bets, what action can one take against him?

A—This appears to come under the normal rule that gambling debts are unenforceable. In other words the bookie cannot be sued for the unpaid winnings.

Q—Is the deposit part of the bookmaker's legal trading assets?

A—In a limited sense, yes. They are assets which are attached exclusively to the trade between the bookie and the person who deposits the money. The money in the deposit account should not, however, be used by the bookie for any other purpose.

Q—Should the deposit be kept separate from the trading account and should this money be returnable on demand by the punter if he wishes to close the account?

A—It should certainly be kept separate in the books of the bookmaker, though it may not be necessary to keep it in a separate bank account. The money should certainly be returnable on demand by the punter unless the agreement between the punter and the bookie indicates otherwise, e.g. on seven days' notice.

Q—Is there any difference between the trading and deposit accounts for solicitors, estate agents or bookmakers or do they all come under the same legal requirements?

A—In principle, a deposit held by a bookie closely resembles clients' money held by solicitors. In reality, however, the situation is very different because solicitors are closely controlled in the way they handle clients' money by Act of Parliament and detailed rules monitored by the Law Society. There are no such professional rules governing bookmakers.

Generally the deposit ought to remain the beneficial property of the punter and the bookmaker simply holds it as a sort of trustee, i.e. for the benefit of the punter.

However, if a bookmaker goes bust and deposit money goes down the drain with him, then the result is simply that the money becomes a debt owed by the bookmaker to the punter and the punter presumably has to claim in the bankruptcy along with the rest of the creditors.

When I arrived the manager told me Mr Higgs had absconded and asked, "What's he owe you?"

"The ten grand Higgins winnings, and what about my three grand cash deposit?" I replied in distress.

The earwigging ginger beard then introduced himself

as a fellow casualty and glumly informed me. "You're one of the lucky ones."

To make matters worse, when I later broke the disastrous news to my part shareholder mate explaining I had been wiped out and it was back to the old job stakes, he just kept repeating, "What about my eight hundred quid - you had the bet for me - do I still get paid out?"

"And what about that bookie in Sible Hedingham?"

"What happened there?" asked John.

"Esal Bookmakers at the time were advertising individual match odds for the Suntory Match Play in the Life and went an unbelievable 5/4 Bobby Clampett to beat Kuramoto. I showed this guy the ad and asked, 'I am a regular punter - can I bet 7/4 - what's the best you can do for the Ol' Bandit then?' When he told me I could bet 13/8 the readies came out of my trouser pocket quicker than Billy the Kid could draw a gun.

'Any chance of the same bet again?' I asked with my £800 tax paid Clampett voucher safely in the bin.

'That'll do,' he told me as I departed to make for the nearest telephone box to bet the widely available 13/8 Kuramoto for the same stake, which would guarantee a profit of £340 whatever the outcome.

When I eventually went back to collect, he told me Esals had made a rick with their odds and he was not going to pay me out. I thought he'd got it into his head an attempt to mug the Ol' Bandit with the odds was worth a try - but when he told me he was binning my stake money the resulting scuffle led to an on-the-deck *five-minute bear hug.*

When I went back a few weeks later, after the Life had arbitrated in my favour, he still wouldn't pay me. I was as sick as a pig because being mugged for my stake money meant I'd ironed out the readies in all departments."

"What happened then?" asked John.

"Well, he was determined to test the Ol' Bandit's bottle to the bitter end and finished up losing his permit and licence in the Magistrates' Court but the funny thing was a few days later he sent me a cheque for the lot."

Life ruling gets bookie banned

AN **ESSEX** bookmaker was refused a betting permit renewal yesterday—because he failed to pay out on a winning bet.

"Cor, you've copped it over the years," sympathised John, intent on hearing more.

"You'll love this one," I promptly continued.

"I found myself in a Walthamstow Betting shop on the Guineas morning of '84 showing the guvnor, John Power, an ad from the previous day's Life, which quoted crazy odds for two of Sunday's league cricket matches.

I was really pleased with myself blagging those two big value singles on Warwicks at Evens and Glamorgan at 2/1 and I had a nifty double, but when I went back Monday morning to collect my Monkey, he refused to pay out and accused me of 'Skullduggery'.

Apparently he was on the phone trying to hedge with Power within minutes of me leaving the shop, but when he was offered drastically reduced odds and told 'it's only the early bird catches the worm', he nearly 'blew a fuse'.

I kept telling him he was the Bookmaker and any bets laid at agreed odds once accepted were his responsibility to honour, but he just kept giving me the 'I'm only a small bookmaker trying to scrape a living' routine with no mention of the shop's mug punters inevitably still doing their dough .

The hassle of ten visits and about fifty quid's worth of petrol later he decided to pay me, after the Life ruled, 'A bookmaker is not bound to bet at list prices offered by another firm, but if he lays such odds he should stand by them."

"Bloody Bookmakers!" groaned the Bandit, well inside the final furlong of the evening's 'Best Bitter 5 fold'. The regimental "time please" order to vacate the bar was the cue to 'crash out', and concluded the evening's review of some disturbing cases taken from the Bandit's extensive Bookmaker Dispute file.

The female early wake up call shook us groggily out of our beds into an ice cold morning. A quick glance out of the window revealed the first hint of sunrise with the car park lights reflecting against rows of frost covered cars. An initial encounter with the elements persuaded us to gather yet further attire before the day's requirements were dumped in the boot.

"Haven't the Life and Post arrived yet?" I anxiously asked the young waitress as we departed from our extended breakfast.

I wouldn't like to guess how many degrees below zero it was that morning, but it took a good twenty minutes of running the car engine and scraping windows before we were able to depart to the Jack Nicklaus designed course just three miles down the road.

"Run for your lives," the Bandit joked as we approached a couple of elderly ticket sellers, bringing them to life. The mock 'Jib-In' was taken in good spirit as we then headed for the score board clutching our four day passes.

We estimated the bet copping a second year in succession to be no bigger than 1/2, but as we approached the scoreboard to view a full complement of one hundred and fifty starters, we seemed to have everything on our side - but what about the weather?

"This is match number 10 - on the tee ..." announced the familiar figure of the official starter suitably attired in his customary blue blazer, to a spectating applause of 'Just Two'.

The field were also being sent off from the 10th tee, but with the star faces not appearing for an hour or so, we decided a quick inspection of the Par Threes was in order.

"Fore" the caddie bellowed at the exposed 14th tee, as the third ball was launched into its misdirected journey towards outer space.

"All odds are subject to fluctuation," joked John peering towards the sky as our Bottle On chance had already been revised to Odds Against.

The bitterly cold, blustery conditions were deteriorating all the time, but we decided to stall up for a while around the green to say our prayers, and funk for the next few groups. An hour later, with my initial quote of 4/5 any named player's ball landing on the green being extended to 9/2, and sensing the danger of hypothermia, we began the paratroopers' hike back to the tented village.

"Let's take a look at the old scoreboard," I gloomily suggested to John as we battled the winds, thankfully well inside the final furlong.

The predicted sea of blue disks displaying the Over Par scores confirmed our view that there was more chance of the course record being broken than of clocking that special yellow disk. Dejected and looking for a live interest, we used our cups of coffee as hand warmers while discussing the possibility of making a move on an already 2 Under Par Langer.

We recalled watching Langer's calamitous start the previous year when - like a greyhound that had turned in the traps - he began his race running backwards, being 8 Over Par after playing just two holes: but he had eventually steamed through the field like an express train, miraculously snatching the tournament third spot.

The clue was there - "Blimey, Langer has just gone Three Under" -"Where's the price wise?" - "What next?" "Hello, is that Stanley Racing?", were the beginnings of my telephone activities that led to a shared value for money Monkey win and a Bottle Place bet at 12/1.

Langer had been started from the 10th tee for the second year in succession and, having purchased the day's quota of telephone adrenalin, we purposefully jogged out towards the 15th hole.

The stress of watching Langer struggle in the worst conditions we had ever witnessed as golf punters was intolerable, but as the leader board was clocked approaching the 18th green, despite being 'checked up' he was still favourably placed and no bets would be cancelled.

Although fully paid up members of the 'Bernard Langer Supporters' Club', we decided to leave him to it for a while, and miserably began to stroll back to the tented village to OD on some more caffeine.

The approaching rear side of the scoreboard made a further pipe obligatory as we began the scan with match number one in the top left hand corner. The pointless exercise seemed near completion as my eyes glided down the final column towards match number 50, but already beginning the trudge to the coffee I found myself zooming back to that final match.

Jay Townsend - who's he?

The Eleventh Hole - 202 yards in this weather - impossible.

Minces on the blink - Very likely.

A rick by one of the score kids - the Jolly.

"Did Jay Townsend get a hole-in-one?" I anxiously asked the Anorak above my head, eyes fixed to the small yellow disk containing the 'screaming red one' only feet away.

"He did - incredible, wasn't it?" came the polite reply, igniting an explosion of euphoria.

"It's in the bin!" I shouted, to the 'Cup winning arms' of an out-of-earshot John. It took a good fifteen minutes to regain our composure before heading for the champagne marquee to begin official celebrations.

"What a result," I repeated to John, beginning my third glass of champers.

"We've really had it off this time - God knows how much we've binned on the singles but the doubles and accers could come to telephone numbers." I feverishly continued to a beaming John.

112

"More champagne, Sir?" asked the ever faithful Jeeves. How could I refuse with our hero Jay Townsend still playing the early stages of his round.

A little known American golfer, his feat would be unlikely to even make the local press, so it was essential to get our hands on some sort of documentary proof to show the bookies when we turned up to collect - so what better than a copy of his scorecard. "The cards should arrive in about twenty minutes - what is it, a hole-in-one again?" the busy female face enquired, completing stall up number four inside the warmth of P.G.A. portable headquarters.

THE
BENSON & HEDGES INTERNATIONAL OPEN

ST. MELLION GOLF & COUNTRY CLUB
18th – 21st April, 1991

Match: 50   Time: 14.00
18 APR 91   Round: 1
..Jay TOWNSEND USA ✓

Tee: 10   84

Hole	Yards	Par	Comp Score	Hole	Yards	Par	Comp Score	Marker's own Score
1	420	4	4	10	448	4	4	
2	543	5	4	11	202	3	1	
3	373	4	5	12	545	5	6	5
4	185	3	4	13	404	4	4	
5	354	4	5	14	174	3	3	
6	430	4	6	15	442	4	6	
7	502	5	5	16	554	5	6	
8	140	3	3	17	456	4	5	
9	410	4		18	472	4	4	
OUT	3357	36	45	IN	3697	36	39	
				OUT	3357	36	45	
				TOTAL	7054	72	84	

MARKER'S SIGNATURE

COMPETITOR'S SIGNATURE

113

The time had progressed to well past 7 pm, and in the Arctic dusk conditions we decided to tackle the eighteenth fairway from green to tee and back, both to kill time and stay alive. We allowed forty five minutes to pass for fear of being banned from the P.G.A. for life on the grounds of being a bloody nuisance, but thank God, when we returned, the busy smiles and the long-awaited presentation of my reserved 'Townsend' score card felt like receiving a priceless scroll.

5. OFFICIAL RESULTS

Saltash Town Centre was the first port of call early the next morning, but the moustache thought I was taking the p*?s when I told him I wanted copies of every national and local newspaper in the shop. The painstaking job of scouring the sports pages was concluded in the car with a final cover-to-cover analysis of the Telegraph making our fifty photocopies of the Townsend scorecard more valuable than ever.

There was the chance of getting a result in the 'Golfweek Magazine' (out Thursday), but failing that, the inevitable Sporting Life (Green Seal Service) confirmation would be published in a week or so - a letter of request was already in the post.

Our late arrival at the course, just in time to catch Langer's second round, had produced improved weather conditions, but yesterday's 1 Over Par 73 had left him three strokes behind leaders Phillip Walton and Faldo. Langer shot a magnificent best of the day 68 to pull himself up to second spot, two adrift of second round leader Walton, but in an eventful third round a disastrous 75 left him proceeding into the final round four strokes behind the new tournament leader Jose Rivero.

"Aye Aye, that's the end," I told John as Langer found himself five strokes off the pace with thirteen to play.

We were not too disappointed, because the

Townsend Hole-in-One, achieved in conditions Golf Weekly magazine later described as "the sternest examination of European Tour Pros for many a year," had not been repeated - but an unexpected Birdie at the 8th appeared to inject renewed inspiration into the never-say-die Langer.

A dejected Rivero at the 13th found himself in all sorts of trouble in a greenside valley, eventually departing with a triple Bogey 7 dropping him from being a shot ahead to two behind a now all-to-play-for Langer.

Singh and Walton playing ahead only increased the tension, with Birdies at the 16th and 17th respectively, but Langer, with a beautiful chip from the back of the green, also made Birdie at 16 to go 1 Under Par, and took the lead by one precious stroke.

At the 18th tee, relieved at witnessing on the distant green Singh's 5 foot Birdie attempt staying above ground, mobile phone preparations for an emergency play off stakes saver were thankfully abandoned. Our enthusiastic dash to the green was rewarded by Langer hitting a brilliant 105 yard sand wedge second shot to within three feet for a memorable Birdie 3, securing the Benson and Hedges title and £66,660 Winner's cheque.

Langer's return from the grave had added a further £7,000 to our Hole-in-One winnings and served only to motivate us even further on our relentless climb up the ladder.

6. CLUSTER BOMB CLUB

11.45 a.m. Monday morning: only five weeks to go 'till the Volvo. "All we need now is no aggro collecting the St. Mellion winnings, then - carry on 'sploding," yelled the Bandit, as we approached the rainbow facade of Southampton's Spectrum Racing.

Spectrum had laid a generous 10/1 the St. Mellion Hole-in-One, but with John only managing to get £60 on, he was not venturing to collect the Crown Jewels.

A face chewed gum amongst an Aladdin's cave of colourful 'Betting Bonus Offers' splattered across the walls. With that priceless Townsend scorecard and winning voucher on standby, the time had arrived to get the first readies of the campaign safely in the bin.

"I didn't think the bet had a chance in hell of copping in that weather," John told him, producing the victorious slip. "I brought this along just in case you had problems confirming the result," he continued, thrusting the Townsend scorecard under the security screen.

"I know Monday can be a bad day for readies - a kite will do if it helps you out, mate," John went on, his eagerness triggering the beginnings of a slip search that was to end some five minutes later as the manager's amicable confusion changed to the look of a man who had discovered bullion from a shipwreck.

"God, this comes to over six hundred quid," he said, sitting down and re-gathering himself.

The inevitable phone call to head office was luckily short and sweet, and thankfully the Guvnor, Bill, had been watching the BBC's television coverage when apparently out of the blue, Peter Allis had announced the incredible news to the world.

Minutes later John found himself being congratulated on his unlikely success, while gleefully accepting his winnings. The manager clearly expected the cash to disappear into the early morning mist forever, but with no visible state changes from the Spectrum Camp, John decided to chance a further play.

"I'm off to the British Open in July - Do you think there's a chance the Guvnor might lay me the same bet again?" he hopefully asked. "I doubt it, mate," came the reply, but a tenner tip encouraged him to promptly make the call.

"No problem mate - have what you like," came the reply. Bill no doubt believed there was little chance lightning would strike twice, and with the manager clearly being told to lay a bet, John found himself faced with the always difficult calculation of how much to stake without the risk of blowing himself out.

"Hundred quid OK?"

"No problem," replied the beaming smile, but when he went on to say that Bill was one of the South's most fearless layers, John felt compelled to proceed with an all out attack. "It's still 10/1 a tournament if I bet doubles?" he enquired, seeking assurance as he counted his windfall. "I don't see why not," the manager responded, proudly handing over one of Spectrum's colourful propaganda leaflets.

THE SOUTH'S LEADING RACING SERVICE

(0273) 220918 (all lines) plus 24 hour service

(We guarantee you won't get better terms or service!)

WE GIVE YOU "UNDISPUTABLY" THE BEST SEAT IN THE HOUSE!

SPORTS BETTING · GREYHOUNDS · SPORTS BETTING · HORSE RACING · SPORTS BETTING

SUNDAY FOR TELE BETTING THE OFFICE IS OPEN	★★★★★	EVENING RACING USUAL FACILITIES

* Personal Attention * S.P. and Board Prices * Weekly Accounts * Ante Post Prices *

OFFICE TELEPHONE LINES OPEN 8.30 a.m. MON. TO SATURDAY AND COVER ALL MAJOR SPORTING EVENTS, WITH 24 HOUR AFTER OFFICE HOURS SERVICE LINE	TO OPEN A CREDIT OR DEPOSIT ACCOUNT LEAVE A DEPOSIT TO-DAY AND BET IN THE COMFORT OF YOUR OWN HOME TO-DAY
ALL PHONE BETS RECEIVED BEFORE 11 a.m. AT ONLY 5p IN THE £1 ON PREPAID TAX BETS p IN THE £1 THEREAFTER ON PREPAID TAX BETS	1/4 ODDS ON ALL HANDICAPS HORSES OR GREYHOUNDS WITH 6 OR MORE RUNNERS 1/4 ODDS ON ALL T.V. RACES C4/B.B.C HORSES OR GREHOUNDS WITH 6 OR MORE RUNNERS
IMMEDIATE SETTLEMENT (SAME DAY OF RACING IF REQUESTED) OR ON A WEEKLY BASIS SAT. TO SAT. A/C MADE UP 8.30 a.m. MON.	ALL TELEPHONE BETS TAPED FOR SECURITY OF CUSTOMERS, AND PLEASE ASK ABOUT OUR BONUSES ON SPECIALITY BETS

Having been put to the test, we have proved that we are the best. So take some good advice and forget the rest !	YOU NAME IT - WE BET ON IT

THE SOUTH'S FIRST 24 HOUR SPORTS BETTING SERVICE

We will guarantee a fast, efficent, friendly service with security and confidentiaiity
BE WELL AHEAD OF THE FIELD by opening an account with:-
'SPECTRUM'S '' RACING SERVICE - leaves others in the stails

What's this - The South's leading bookmakers ... three branches ... Security, Integrity and peace of mind assured ... and ... blimey, a £100,000 limit!

John's body entered into a shiver of excitement as he made his way to the Spectrum slips to begin the task of scratching out half a dozen of £50 doubles.

"Each double returns six grand — Yeah! That's right, Bill, six grand," John heard the manager say before his unease changed to relief as each bet was rung through the till.

John began to fantasize about his trip back with Securicor in September - and those wonderful January days when he would be sunbathing in the Paddock at Florida's Gulfstream Park Racecourse without a worry in the world apart from the day's 'Pick 6' challenge.

"I might as well play up my winnings," John was soon saying, as the sight of more doubles and another 'carpet' caused the first noticeable 'sweat up,' but after a flustered call on the 'Bill hotline' he thankfully had six more vouchers to add to his now valuable collection.

The potential winnings if all doubles copped was £72,000 but - wait a minute - the shop limit was £100,000. To really finish the Spectrum organisation off for good the answer had to be trebles, but carbon copies displaying three tournaments at 10/1 would be as rare as a nugget to a 'This is my last day out here' gold prospector.

John's trebles construction was suddenly interrupted by the manager who was becoming curious about this apparent obession to splodge on Hole-in-Ones. "Bloody good bet, that," he whispered as John made sure the US Open - British Open - European Open treble had not been duplicated.

"I usually punt on the tournament players, but this lot will give me an interest for the rest of the season," John said. "What's happening now?" asked the agitated head peering over his shoulder. "Just scratching out a few tenner trebles before I shoot off," John replied, shrugging his shoulders. "No trebles - the Guvnor said 'No trebles'," the manager positively said before the bleeping phone prompted a withdrawal.

John reverted to doubles attack, choosing to ignore the gloomy stare, but when the manager suddenly charged towards him screaming "No more - no more!" he really thought he was in trouble.

Alarm bells ringing, John reflected back to the 'Welsh Valley Skirmish' a few years back when the Bandit, delighted at betting a thirty three ponies, made haste from the shop only to be confronted by that '6/4 and get lost' Gorilla from up the hill. "He's had you over, Evans, you dim bastard," he said as the Bandit found himself being frogmarched back into the shop for a refund.

The nightmare that Spectrum would attempt to call all bets off thankfully did not materialise as John was frantically told "Bill's got too involved and wants to button up". He asked if his bets qualified for Spectrum's '20% doubles Bonus' as he prepared to leave, but a shake of the head was both the answer and the goodbye as John sprinted back to the car.

"Seventy two grand," was all he needed to say as the Bandit feverishly flicked through the Spectrum Wad.

"They thought St Mellion was a fluke, and they're certain they've nicked back their six hundred quid," he excitedly explained as we began the journey back to Castle Bromwich.

Despite doing quite well during the early days of the campaign, Spectrum had been the South's 'Oddball' with only St. Mellion winnings to collect, but thanks to John they had now become fully paid up members of the 'Cluster Bomb Club'.

7. THE FIRST READIES IN THE BIN!

Tuesday, 11.25 a.m. South West Birmingham. "Where's it say hole-in-one?", the stubborn bookie blasted, as his heavily tattooed arm wiped away deposits of white froth while John pinpointed the 'shot of the week article'. "The first ace of the tournament - that doesn't mean he got a hole-in-one", he spluttered, as John reinforced his efforts with the Townsend scorecard. "You should try using Tipp-Ex," he then said, vigorously stabbing a finger at the 11th hole alteration excuse.

The 'yet to sink in that I've done three grand' bookie remained resolute as John persevered with his claim.

"I've had a straightforward winning bet and I want to be paid," he insisted, now supplying a list of telephone confirmation sources including a 'Tell 'em you're a subscriber' warning regarding the Press Association. "Call back later," he arrogantly snarled, compelling John to take an early lunch, but any optimism went out the window when he returned only to find himself in a 'don't push me over the edge man' confrontation. "There was no bloody hole-in-one - if you don't believe me, ask Hills yourself," he raged. "Why ask Hills when you've got that lot?" John asked, pointing to the array of documentary evidence, knowing full well the bookie hadn't enquiried beyond the telephonist. "They know everything, and besides all bookies pay out by the Sporting Life," came the reply. "I don't want us to fall out over this, mate," John told him, hoping last Friday's letter to the Life was receiving prompt attention. "I've got work to do," the bookie snapped back, withdrawing to the sanctuary of his desk. "No sweat, I'll call back later," yelled John as he breezed away from the smirk of disinterest. "We should get paid," he assured the Bandit, as they drove through the flooded potholes of O'Shanters car park. "Stall up stakes?" I enquired. "He knows he's done his dough, but the Life should do the trick," John assured me as we headed North to Leicester on the edge of the Arthur Whittaker fall out zone.

<u>Leicester, three hours later.</u>

"There was no chance of a press up, but at least he'd taken the trouble to check the bet out," he enthused, busily stuffing B J Racing's £2,100 into the Barclays Bank 'Hole-in-One' collection bag. "Better get moving," screamed a delighted Bandit, as the Meter Maid's sagging boat encouraged a prompt departure.

"Get the next one in the bin and we'll be flying," blurted John, as we raced towards Nottingham, hopefully to the pleasure of collecting a 'Coleman Commissions' late afternoon £5,000 payout.

"That were catch bet," he found himself being told by the downcast owner. "A Hole-in-One's a bloody even money chance," he gloomily mumbled on. "I only got the idea from a golf magazine," John boldly replied in defence. "What's your name?" he then solemnly asked, rocking John back on his heels.

The sight of the twiddling pen and cheque book brought much relief as John realised his splutterings onto a Coleman kite was now a must. John was barely able to disguise his elation as the owner despondently disposed of five large. "Don't come back," came his unsportsmanlike goodbye, with his expression dispelling all thoughts of producing the Beaumont Girl 'refund' voucher.

The Hole-in-One roadshow was now on megadrive as we made our way back to base camp, laughing into the sunset as we recited memorable extracts from the doubters in the game - you're wasting your time, all the Big Odds went years ago - I schlapped round every bookie in Swindon and never got a Dino on - Drove myself mad for a week in Stafford and left the Ex's behind.

<u>Wednesday, 9.34 a.m. Midland Bank Nottingham</u>.

"What do you mean it still takes two days and costs a tenner?" cried John as he enquiried about 'Express Clearance' due to last night's nightmare vision of a Coleman change of heart.

The chaos of street maps, files, betting slips and itinerary sheets, together with our sense of urgency, made it feel we were taking part in a rally, and with Townsend's 'Ace' being more widespread than anticipat,ed John opened the car's locker for a third time to stuff readies in the collection bag.

Nottingham's street map had been acquired in booklet form and with the use of coloured marker pens the most economical route to each bookie had been painstakingly preplanned.

We were ahead of schedule and flying as we drove towards Rubble Racing but the Ol' Bandit appeared unsettled at the prospect of collecting our £16,000 because when a bookie irons out that sort of dough - anything can happen.

The approaching black haze transformed into a familiar facade of super heroes signifying the return of Del Duffer!

The blaring sounds of the SIS in-action broadcast welcomed me back into familiar surroundings, which but for the prominence of the Rubble Racing Logo, could have been Ladbrokes.

I wandered towards a band of punters glued to the early stages of Kempton's 1.30 race, glancing at the beard inside mission control - was this the bespectacled pinstripe I once knew? - Resolute that with sixteen large at stake I had to be assertive from the word go - the hare was now running and action about to commence.

"I'll lay 5/4 Snowtown Boy," I bellowed, enthralled in the climax but only too aware that the ploy would draw his attention. "Aye Aye - call a copper - Out of Jail!" then came my frenzied victory scream as I stood on a stool with clenched fist and arm erect, now the centre of attention.

My focus returned to the rising 'beard' now staring intently. "Whey Hey - trying to take on the Ol'

Bandit at the golf game," I screamed, bounding towards him. "Mike done you a favour," I gleefully continued, launching the winning tickets into mission control. "What's the spread on punters at the Wick today guv? - it's $15^1/_2$ - $17^1/_2$ with me," I went on, pointing to the 1.48 p.m. 3/1 each of six betting show with intentions of smothering any reply. "You f*!?*d me, you f*!?*d me," he angrily told me, looking like he'd seen happier days. "Who laid 66/1?" he then wanted to know. "Doug Poultney of South London," I honestly replied. "What's he, on the dole now?" he fired back.

"Don't worry, guv, I'll give you a chance to get a few quid back," I assured him as I began a victory lap of the shop. "I'm going to have an Odds On 8 Timer but it only works out at 9/2 to my readies," I screamed, buzzing round the walls' prominence of snooker betting.

Ignoring my performance, his bad tempered rummage through desk drawers provided a positive clue. "I make it fifteen and a half grand with the cricket, guv," I then shouted, seeking assurance, but a sighting of his cheque book prompted my return to mission control.

My many years of study in the specialised field of bookmaker psychology told me a consoling job was in order. "A readies injection for the Ol' Bandit after last night's great Hall Green dogs disaster," I beamed as I was informed my cheque was being postdated for next Thursday. "I was doing about five grand by the seventh race," I resolutely continued, "ended up betting a seven and a half thousand to five for a three quarter get out and the Ol' Bandit got done a short head."

"I'm paying you out, mate, but only because I know you can take my permit," came the whinging response.

Jublilantly stuffing my kite in my bin, there was little value in reprisal as I left the broken figure of a man who had made the big mistake of taking on the Ol' Bandit - Match Play.

"What chance have this lot got with us?" yelled the Bandit, already speeding towards the next bookie. "We're in the Premier Division - the rest are in the Beazer League," he then crowed. "That makes it twenty one grand," beamed John. "Forget about money," snapped the Bandit. "Every grand in the bin is another point for us in the punting European Order of Merit."

Thursday 9.20 a.m.

I had sensed that all was not well when it was insisted that I return the next morning at precisely 9.30 a.m, regarding a three grand St. Mellion collection - but as the fluorescent light sucked me through the door, my stomach was soon rolling when the blue uniform the grim face and note pad meant - Blimey, it's the BILL !

"That's him," the bookie timidly whispered.
"What's all this about?" I asked, determined not to be intimidated by the unexpected welcome.
"You know full well you conned me with those

bloody golf bets," he jumped - bravado supplied by the arm of the law. "

"What's it all about?" I asked again.

"I mean that bloody piece of paper."

I had remembered feeling like Indiana Jones plucking those Golf Ante Post Special sheets promoting 14/1 hole in one odds out of a remote betting shop somewhere in South Wales, some three years ago. The priceless scrolls had unfortunately all but perished due to extensive use, but with just one still intact, I prayed that disintegration could be deferred until the British Open.

"What's that got to do with anything?" I fumed.

"You printed that bloody sheet yourself and told me you'd had 25/1 and bigger from other bookies," I stood accused.

"Mr Potter," the police officer interrupted, entering the proceedings.

"It's not my duty, Sir," he assertively continued, now speaking to me, "to get involved in any dispute between Mr Potter and yourself - but it has been suggested it might be sensible if we keep an eye on proceedings while the matter is being resolved." The old bill thus declared their intention to participate only as referee if required.

"It's not just me that copped it, officer," then barked the bookie. "He's conned everybody round here," he rattled on. "I've built up a reputation over the past 20 years of giving my punters a fair deal, and provide a valuable service to the local community," began the bail out speech. "That's right, isn't it, Herbert?" he wormed, ignored by the Demob overcoat gliding past like a ghost.

"I'm going to pay you out three grand for your St. Mellion bet," he then growled, as I purposefully retained my composure, relieved that he wasn't going to have a crack at knocking me for the lot.

"But those doubles," he continued, referring to my cocktail of death, "they're void, and you get your stake money back." Elastic bands and readies were rummaged for, then produced on the counter.

"No wonder you invited the old bill in for a cup of tea," I fumed in response.

"My rules state," he ground on, "If the odds aren't correct, and you know as well as I do 20/1 weren't the correct odds, I'm entitled to void the bet."

"You're the bloody bookmaker," I furiously blasted back. "I didn't point a shotgun at your head and make you lay the bet, did I?" began my defence. "You can't cancel my bets just because you feel like it," I angrily told him. "If the lot had got beat, would you have tracked me down and returned my stake money?" I raged on.
"You're a f*!+?!g con artist," was all he could say.

In stepped the Bill. "Language," he warned.

"I'm not standing for this," I said, alert to the fact that my three grand was not yet in the bin. "How would you feel if a stroke like this was pulled on you?" I continued, but I began to realise I had no choice other than to swallow.

"Give me my three grand," I snapped, as again I suffered another mugger masquerading as a bookmaker, but realised pursuing the matter further would be folly because screams or any mention of Holes-In-One might bring the campaign to a premature conclusion. By Friday evening £40,000 had been extracted from the East Midlands bookies, and apart from a detour to the O'Shanter pub car park for another three grand, we were all set for a Monday morning onslaught on the Liverpool area.

8. OPERATION CUMBRIAN STORM

The invasion of Liverpool and its surrounding suburbs was the beginning of four weeks of solid grafting in the North West. Basing ourselves in Chester, the prime objective was to cluster-bomb Scouse bookies as speedily as possible.

It had taken many hours of concentration inside Ilford Library to prepare the Merseyside Itinerary. Hours of wading through huge volumes of Yellow Pages, plotting economical routes through a spider web of City back streets, not to mention the dreaded pub and Labour Club run from Warrington to Birkenhead.

Three days of grey skies and drizzle didn't deter our plans to hit the heartland of Liverpool, but with only a dozen ten and twenty quid singles averaging around 20/1 for the Volvo and US Open as our reward, and realising many Scouse bookies were penniless, the intended 'Cluster Bet' onslaught now appeared unlikely to materialise. Anyway, only a fool would set up big liabilities with skint bookies and hope to land the double of the bet coping - and getting paid out.

<u>Liverpool Shlapathon - Day 4</u>

Ye Olde Edwardian Country house at this peaceful rural village certainly didn't look like a betting shop, but a sign on the main gates, reading 'Licenced

Betting Premises - This Way' enticed the Bandit to walk the pebbled driveway before more directions led to quarters at the rear.

"It's 5p in the Pound," the posh lady enthused as I entered premises reminiscent of a refurbished Ladbrokes. "Don't you agree, it's grand racing over the sticks today?" she continued, refusing air.

"Well, actually, I'm more of a golfer myself," came my reply. I thought she would be more familiar with Hickstead than Hexham. I continued, "I had a strange bet last year on any player scoring a Hole-in-One at odds of 66/1 in the Volvo PGA, so is it only horses and dogs or are golf bets allowed?"

"There are no odds quoted in today's Sporting Life, but it all sounds frightfully interesting," she then frothed. "Hubby's secretary of our local club - I'll give him a ring, he'll know." She picked up the phone and dialled.

"Aye say, Stafford, it's Hilary," the conversation began. "There's a young man here requesting odds for a hole-in-one who tells me he received 66/1 last year."

... please turn up the volume, I begged silently.

"That's what I thought." The mumblings went on for a while before her attentions returned to me.

"Stafford suggests 80/1 - would that be acceptable?" she now politely asked.

"Sounds fair to me," I replied.

She returned to the telephone. "Yes, he's happy

Stafford, and by the way - this evenings 'Pheasant Dianne' is Orf!"

The numbers game had really paid off here, with us being rewarded with £25 Hole-in-One singles on the remaining banker events, but with only two weeks left until the Volvo P.G.A. at Wentworth, we now urgently needed to find a new base camp central to the North West.

* Large Deluxe Swimming Pool
* Central Location
* Fitness Centre
* French Cuisine

Lancaster's Post House Hotel would be the place for us as, we promptly commenced 'Operation Cumbrian Storm'.

Our initial mission was a military style clockwise sweep across the hills and dales, ruthlessly ferreting out small bookies in remote villages, but when we clocked a primeval-looking betting shop painted in colours belonging to one of the biggest bookmaking groups in the North, we were staggered. The whole area looked as though the sheep outnumbered the people by 100 to 1.

Surrey Racing's usual phrase when closing one's account is 'economically unviable'. It certainly seemed to apply here, but the mystery of the bookie's presence was an irrelevance as the Bandit steadfastly pumped himself up to play yet another hand.

"Is it only horses and dogs you bet on, or can I

have a splodge on the golf?" I soon found myself asking an uninterested Scots face, wishing it had been practical to play a cassette recording of my opening line.

"Aye," came the listless reply.

"I had a bet on a hole-in-one in the British Open last year at another branch and got 16/1," I bashed on - well, where's the harm in an occasional white lie?

"You were robbed, lad," came the reply, my odd-ball request igniting the motor.

"Can you get me odds for any player to hole-in-one during the Volvo PGA tournament at Wentworth in a couple of weeks?" I now asked, clutching my tournament dates information sheet just in case.

"That's any player?" he mumbled back, already dialling H.Q., but the in-play boatometer clue made it about Even Money that his next word to me would be Evens.

"You're going to be disappointed, lad," came the ominous response. However, when he went on to say they were 'only' prepared to lay 10/1, the ground began to tremble under my feet.

An assortment of Farmers and Codgers, already well tuned into proceedings, made me feel uncomfortable as I grappled with one of two grand wads of fifties stuffed into my jean pockets.

If only I could somehow get a chunk on, this

substantial group would probably pay out without too much screaming, but the big fear was old Scotsman phoning my bets through to H.Q. for confirmation.

"This'll win doing hand stands," I told him, sliding in a hundred quid Hole-in-One bet together with the same stake on trap 6 at the 'Wick'.
The 'sweetener' ploy appeared to work, as both bets were promptly accepted: all interest was now on the dog race.

"It doesn't matter what I do," I declared as five baulked six out of contention. "Whether it's dogs, horses or Gaelic Football - I just keep doing my cobblers," I rambled on, palms now glued to my cheeks in dismay. Mumblings regarding the size of my recent losses were rife as I presented the Scotsman with a further hundred quid Hole-in-One offering - which, to my delight, was accepted without even the slightest fuss.

Available data told me to carry on pumping, and although terrified of a Scotsman-to-H.Q. phone call, I boldly began shooting two £100 Hole-in-One slips in his direction.

You could have turned the gawking audience upside down and given them a good shake, and be struggling to rake up ten quid in coins, so it was hard to understand the psychology of the Scotsman's resolute stand, which kept going until the bulge in my pocket had dwindled into oblivion.

* £2,000 at 10/1, comes to twenty large.

YET there's a chance he'll still take more.

ONLY the tank's disappeared - but what about the Access Card?

NatWest Branch - 26 Miles Away

"I must have your mother's maiden name," the teenage cashier was now insisting. "Your date of birth and previous address just ain't sufficient," she stubbornly went on, as my feverishness to promptly invest my five grand credit limit became difficult to disguise.

The two grand in the tank cock up was a real sickener, because when attempting to resplodge there was a possibility they would try to call the bets off: but with definite chances to set up a super deluxe £70,000 payday, I was prepared to take the risk.

The scurry of security and glancing eyes during the transaction could be compared to trudging past a row of airport customs officers with well over your cigarette allowance, but the handing over of two sealed wads of readies apparently gave the all clear regarding Flexible Friend flimping suspicions.

Epilogue ...

"They didnae want to take any more," the distraught Scotsman bawled, responding to my further Hole-in-One enquiry. "Naw, they didnae want to take any more," he told me again. I assumed that the company had not given him a pat on the back.

Thankfully there was no Hole-in-One bail-out aggravation, but I thought it tactful to leave the scene then, hoping I would soon return to inflict a devastating £20,000 fine.

9. THE PENNY DROPS FOR THE BOOKMAKERS

<u>One Week until Wentworth</u>

We flew through the North and South Manchester itinerary sheets like Speedy Gonzales, averaging 25 shops a day and determined to reach our £½ million target. Manchester bookies love a chat on the old dog and bone, with the result that many Hole-in-One enquires now meant 6/4.

A clued-up bookie is an unpredictable and indeed sometimes dangerous animal; keeping our bottle was an absolute must. Our diligence and courage was to be rewarded with further potential winnings of £70,000, including two individual bets of one hundred pounds at 50/1.

With the sun already high in the sky, and with no bookmaker confrontations planned for the day, we were in good spirits as we tucked into breakfast. We were then to drive back to London for the following day's crucial Wentworth action, but while the Life was receiving its first workout, our mood was to take a change.

Clued up Scottish bookies 'Trevino' had hit on the bright idea of advertising Hole-in-One odds at 7/4. Our hearts sank as we considered the effect of the ad on its bookmaker readership.

We faced two problems - firstly, if they had laid

excessive Hole-in-One odds, there might be screams when we tried to collect. Secondly, future Hole-in-One enquiry conversion statistics could plummet.

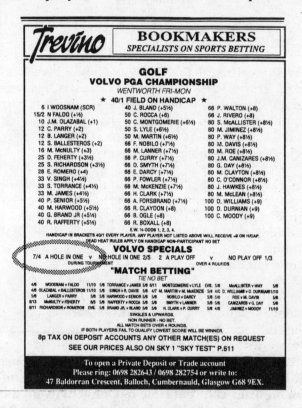

Trevino

BOOKMAKERS

SPECIALISTS ON SPORTS BETTING

GOLF

VOLVO PGA CHAMPIONSHIP

WENTWORTH FRI-MON

★ 40/1 FIELD ON HANDICAP ★

6	I WOOSNAM (SCR)	40	J. BLAND (+5½)	66	P. WALTON (+8)
15/2	N FALDO (+½)	50	C. ROCCA (+6)	66	J. RIVERO (+8)
10	J.M. OLAZABAL (+1)	50	C. MONTGOMERIE (+6½)	80	S. McALLISTER (+8½)
12	C. PARRY (+2)	50	S. LYLE (+6½)	80	M. JIMINEZ (+8½)
12	B. LANGER (+2)	50	M. MARTIN (+6½)	80	P. WAY (+8½)
12	S. BALLESTEROS (+2)	66	F. NOBILO (+7½)	80	M. DAVIS (+8½)
16	M. McNULTY (+3)	66	M. LANNER (+7½)	80	M. ROE (+8½)
25	D. FEHERTY (+3½)	66	P. CURRY (+7½)	80	J.M. CANIZARES (+8½)
25	S. RICHARDSON (+3½)	66	D. SMYTH (+7½)	80	G. DAY (+8½)
28	E. ROMERO (+4)	66	E. DARCY (+7½)	80	M. CLAYTON (+8½)
33	V. SINGH (+4½)	66	P. FOWLER (+7½)	80	C. O'CONNOR (+8½)
33	S. TORRANCE (+4½)	66	M. McKENZIE (+7½)	80	J. HAWKES (+8½)
33	M. JAMES (+4½)	66	H. CLARK (+7½)	80	M. McLEAN (+8½)
40	P. SENIOR (+5½)	66	A. FORSBRAND (+7½)	100	D. WILLIAMS (+9)
40	M. HARWOOD (+5½)	66	R. CLAYDON (+8)	100	D. DURNIAN (+9)
40	G. BRAND JR (+5½)	66	B. OGLE (+8)	100	C. MOODY (+9)
40	R. RAFFERTY (+5½)	66	R. BOXALL (+8)		

E.W. ¼ ODDS 1, 2, 3, 4.

HANDICAP IN BRACKETS 40/1 EVERY PLAYER. ANY PLAYER NOT LISTED ABOVE WILL RECEIVE +9 ON H/CAP.

DEAD HEAT RULES APPLY ON HANDICAP NON-PARTICIPANT NO BET

VOLVO SPECIALS

7/4 A HOLE IN ONE v NO HOLE IN ONE 2/5   2 A PLAY OFF v NO PLAY OFF 1/3

DURING TOURNAMENT   OVER 4 ROUNDS

"MATCH BETTING"

TIE NO BET

4/6	WOOSNAM v FALDO	11/10	5/6	TORRANCE v JAMES	5/6	8/11	MONTGOMERIE v LYLE	EVS.	5/6	McALLISTER v WAY	5/6
4/6	OLAZABAL v BALLESTEROS	11/10	5/6	SINGH v R. DAVIS	5/6	4/7	M. MARTIN v M. McKENZIE	5/4	4/6	D. WILLIAMS v D. DURNIAN	11/10
5/6	LANGER v PARRY	5/6	5/6	HARWOOD v SENIOR	5/6	5/6	NOBILO v DARCY	5/6	5/6	ROE v M. DAVIS	5/6
8/13	McNULTY v FEHERTY	6/5	5/6	RAFFERTY v ROCCA	5/6	5/6	SMYTH v LANNER	5/6	5/6	CANIZARES v G. DAY	5/6
8/11	RICHARDSON v ROMEROS	EVS.	5/6	BRAND JR. v BLAND	5/6	5/6	H. CLARK v P. CURRY	5/6	4/6	JIMINEZ v MOODY	11/10

SINGLES & UPWARDS.
NON RUNNER - NO BET.
ALL MATCH BETS OVER 4 ROUNDS.
IF BOTH PLAYERS FAIL TO QUALIFY LOWEST SCORE WILL BE WINNER.

8p TAX ON DEPOSIT ACCOUNTS ANY OTHER MATCH(ES) ON REQUEST

SEE OUR PRICES ALSO ON SKY 1 "SKY TEST" P.611

To open a Private Deposit or Trade account
Please ring: 0698 282643 / 0698 282754 or write to:
47 Baldorran Crescent, Balloch, Cumbernauld, Glasgow G68 9EX.

THE SPORTING LIFE - THURSDAY 23 MAY 1991.

... As news broke of Wraith Grant's second-day elation at the 5th Hole, countless bookies who had laid odds of up to 100/1 would now be regretting their generosity, but that 'Trevino' advertisement was causing us much anxiety.

WENTWORTH CLUB
West Course

24th, 25th, 26th and 27th May 1991

COM	Match: 30		Time: 12.20
MATE	25 MAY 91 .		. Round: 2
	. .Wraith GRANT Eng		
	Tee: 1	71 68 139. ✓	

Marker's own Score	Hole	Yards	Metres	Par	Comp Score	Hole	Yards	Metres	Par	Comp Score	Marker's own Score
4	1	471	431	4	5	10	186	170	3	3	3
3	2	155	142	3	4	11	376	344	4	4	4
5	3	452	413	4	5	12	483	442	5	4	4
4	4	501	458	5	5	13	441	403	4	4	3
3	5	191	175	3	1	14	179	164	3	4	3
4	6	344	314	4	4	15	466	426	4	4	5
3	7	399	365	4	3	16	380	347	4	4	4
3	8	398	364	4	3	17	571	522	5	4	3
4	9	450	411	4	4	18	502	459	5	5	
33	OUT	3361	3073	35	32	IN	3584	3277	37	36	
						OUT	3361	3073	35	32	
						TOTAL	6945	6350	72	68	

MARKER'S SIGNATURE

COMPETITOR'S SIGNATURE

The Dunhill British Masters, held at the Woburn Golf and Country Club, was to commence the following Thursday, but Hole-in-One activity on this event had been kept to an absolute minimum, due to poor statistics and only one hundred and twenty players taking part.

The third banker tournament was to be the US Open a week later. It was held that year at Hazeltine National, Chaska, Minnesota, and we decided to postpone Volvo collections and return to Manchester, but despite Dunhill 7/4 'Trevino' horrors, we continued with moderate success.

The Sporting Life US Open issue, 13 June 1991, as if you hadn't guessed, included further 7/4 announcements:

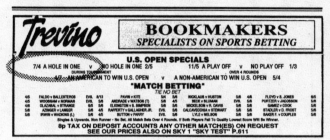

and if that wasn't enough, Golf Correspondent, Jeremy Chapman was suggesting the offer as the pick of the speciality bets.

PICK OF THE SPECIALITY BETS

● Craig Parry 33-1 for Top Non–American (Corals and Surrey)
● Ian Baker-Finch evens to beat Fred Couples (Hills)
● 7-4 a hole in one during the week (Trevino)
● Olazabal 6-4 to beat Ballesteros (Trevino)
● Nick Price 5-6 to beat Ronan Rafferty (Surrey)
● Rocco Mediate 5-6 to beat Jodie Mudd (Victor Chandler)
● Hale Irwin 5-6 to beat Corey Pavin (Victor Chandler)

Estimating the extent of the damage was impossible, but we prayed it wouldn't be the Kiss of Death.

An electrifying roar from Sky's Open coverage that evening was followed by news that the first Ace of the tournament had been achieved by John

143

Inman at the 194yd 4th hole.

Celebrations included mathematical calculations, then discussions, regarding Trevino aggravation permutations: but chunks won, and with the Crown Jewels still to come, a ceasefire was decided.

10.THE ANTICIPATED NIGHTMARE

The beginnings of a Rumble in the bookmaking jungle could be heard, but adequate press coverage of John Inman's triumph had helped to reduce our feelings of unease regarding collections - in stark contrast to the previous year's US Open fiasco, as the Bandit recalls ...

I had endured a horrendous morning visiting the bookies around the fishing town of Hull, getting the same dismal responses I had heard a thousand times before.

Earlier, while driving from my hotel, I had been listening to a cassette by American success coach Tony Robbins, to help psych me up for the day ahead: but with England's one-time brave and fearless bookies screaming: "If William Hill don't bet on it - we don't," or "I'll phone around later and try and get a price," and a way above average number of 6/4 quotes, despite the therapy I felt in danger of cracking up.

With the time fast approaching 1.00 pm, I found myself deep in the maze of an enormous housing estate, still searching for the next bookie on my itinerary. Rarely a day-time drinker, but in desperate need of a leak, the sight of the conspicuously run-down Pig and Whistle lured me into the crowded lounge bar.

Attempting to make for the exit, after being forced to stare at grey flaking walls, the camouflage of cloth caps and suits dismally failed as I heard the dreaded words, "Hey you! What do you want to drink?"

I took my unwanted orange juice over to the threadbare but only seat available, feeling I had just spent 90p on taking a leak. I dreaded to think what pleasures awaited the Public Bar punters, as I prepared to give my Sporting Life the day's second work out.

The old codger I found pitched in next to me with his mouth locked open appeared totally absorbed in the racing pages of The Sun. The clue prompted me to ask if he had any idea where the nearest bookie might be located.

The Odds On chance obliged as he began to describe a small shed type building that was apparently situated outside in the car park. Refreshed and once again ready to commence battle I found myself enduring a lecture, spoken with much feeling, about the perils of gambling and why anyone who frequents any betting shop is an absolute mug, but his words, once translated, got the message across clearly enough - over the years he had done his absolute cobblers at the game.

Ten minutes later I found myself facing what looked more like a large dog kennel than the garden shed I had been told to expect. In order to make sure it looked like one deluxe mug punter had just arrived in town, I placed a now battered Sporting

Life into my jacket pocket. I thought it would have been far more appropriate to have had the name 'Rover' above the front door, rather than the amateurishly stencilled 'Licensed Betting Premises' as my entrance was welcomed by the echoing ring of the shop blower in what appeared to be a condemned area.

A quick scan of the decor revealed countless old issues of the Sporting Life stapled to every spare inch of wall space, with the conspicuous exception of a wallchart quoting odds for the final twenty four contenders in the Greyhound Derby. If I didn't have any success with the Hole-in-One bet, there was always a chance I could bet the new favourite already in the final at 10/1.

Confronted by a grubby, bearded character who looked at least a 7/2 chance to be the owner, my enthusiastic, "Hello, mate," did little to improve his vacant expression. "What's happened to all the punters?" I asked. He confined his reply to pointing a finger at the pub next door.

"It's just as well I turned up then," I continued, failing in my attempt to draw even the slightest smile. He began to explain that all the shop regulars were next door getting legless but usually slid in one by one during the afternoon.

When attempting to place Hole-in-One bets, a frequently used tactic is called 'The Sweetener'. This involves placing a small bet on absolutely anything at current or even under the odds with your potential victim before asking him to quote odds for a Hole-in-One. I had been using Freddie Couples, my hunch for the U.S. Open, for this purpose throughout the previous fortnight, but having decided I did not wish to set foot on the premises again unless I had a good few quid to draw, I decided against using this tactic.

I braced myself to crash straight in with the usual patter, and began to explain that around this time last year in the U.S. Open, I had placed a bet with another bookie on any player scoring a Hole-in-One and had been laid 14/1.

Looking at me as if I were out of my mind for even considering such a bet, he interrupted to point to some newspaper investment, explaining that if I could find any of the big bookies advertising odds he would lay me a bet.

After one slow lap of scrutinising the shop walls and then explaining with a puzzled frown that no Hole-in-One odds could be found, I asked, "Surely if you're a bookmaker you can rake me up some sort of a price?"

"I'm not gaffer, mate," he replied. "governor's in't Public Bar next door. If you really want to bet on t'hole-in-one, why don't you go and have a word with him?"

"What's he look like?" I asked.

"You can't miss him, mate," he assured me, "he's bald, overweight and by now he'll have a good few jars down him so you'll hear him if you don't see him."

Clued up already that a visit to the public bar would not be like lunch at the Savoy, I wished I'd brought along my gas mask as I battled my way through thick layers of smoke. Despite shrieks of bad language from one quarter alerting me to three definite contenders, I decided my best bet was to ask the barman. Eventually catching his attention he pointed towards a crowded table and shouted with a coarse Yorkshire accent, "Over there mate, he's great fat git sittin' in t'corner."

Deciding there was no point in messing about, I approached the rowdy party. Amongst the group of about eight, I didn't need any scales to tell me which one was the bookie. He was seated with his back to me, and staring at his greasy collar, I tapped him on the shoulder. He was temporarily silenced and now staggered to his feet. I found myself enduring a first close up. His bloated face and bulging eyes appeared saturated in sweat. Clearly smashed out of his brain, he spluttered, "How can I help you, son?"

I began to explain that his shop manager had suggested I come and have a word with him, because around this time last year I had placed a bet with a London bookie on any player to Hole-in-One in the U.S. Open Golf.

"What odds did you get?" he interrupted. "They weren't big odds, 14/1," I replied. Puzzled at first, his brain appeared to suddenly shoot into overdrive as he looked towards one of his drinking associates.

"Fred, I've got a bloke here who wants a price for a hole-in-one," he shouted with an arrogant smile, "What odds do you think I should offer?" "If you ask me what's a fair price I'd say if you offered 100/1, you'd be turning him over," came the reply.

The response from the rest of the group included shouts of, "the last time that happened was when that Japanese 'Aoki' won a house but that was donkey's years ago." "God, it's got to be at least a thousand to one chance," and "It never happens."

He clearly thought Christmas had come early and the unexpected donation I was about to make would no doubt be beer money for the next few days.

Turning towards me he asked, "How much do you want to bet?" "Fifty quid, if that's OK," I replied. Placing both hands on my shoulders, he boastfully shouted, "Son, you've got yourself a bet - but I'll offer no more than 14/1." He then grabbed my Sporting Life, on which he scribbled a short note for me to show the manager confirming his permission to lay the bet.

Following pats on the back and a departing handshake that lasted well over a minute, no doubt to once again show his thanks for the donation, I quickly dashed back to the shop, sound in the knowledge that John and myself made the odds for an Ace at Medinah no bigger than a Two/On chance. I could not help but recall the words of flamboyant

bookmaker/gambler John Banks, "Sound advice is invaluable."

The manager, shaken out of his daydream by my return, waffled, "How did you make out, mate?"

"The chief said he would lay me fourteen fifties but asked me to give you this message," I replied, stuffing my Life through the counter bars. Staring at me as if I definitely had a screw loose, without further fuss he rang the bet through the till, scratching his initials next to those 14/1 odds. Briskly walking towards the door, praying nobody was suddenly going to change their minds regarding the transaction, I shortly found myself driving away, hoping my earlier bad luck was now well behind me.

The 1990 U.S. Open was taking place at the

Medinah Golf and Country Club near Chicago, USA, which coincided with the annual Pro-celebrity Golf Tournament at Moor Park near Rickmansworth, where we intended to relax after creating a potential bumper payday with the Deadly Bet. The most reliable way to find out if anyone has Holed-in-One in an American tournament is to get your hands on the telephone number of the 'Press Centre'.

Chicago time being six hours behind ours, my Thursday early evening dialling of the 0101 number resulted in a pleasant American lady breaking the grim news that so far nobody had Holed-in-One.

At the end of Friday's play the half way cut would be made, reducing the field by about half for the final two days. If the ball hadn't dropped into the cup by then, our original Two/On chance would have become definite Odds Against, so tension prior to Friday's late night phone call was considerable.

The second dialling of the 0101 number felt a little like pressing my teletext handset to find out the latest score after having a major splodge on a snooker match. The friendly reply, "Medinah Press Centre," was interrupted by my optimistic, "Would you be kind enough to give me the name of the player who holed in one today, please."

John, who had been nervously pacing the length of my living room, smiled just for a second at my bold request, but the expected reply came only seconds later.

"Sir, there was no hole-in-one today," but after a pause she continued, "I'm sure someone got one yesterday though, if you give me just a second I'll check it out on my computer."

John had picked up on my sudden look of disbelief and was buzzing around the phone sensing the possibility of some good news. I prayed to the gods for a result until she at last returned. "Sir, I can confirm that Jay Don Blake holed in one yesterday at the 9th hole, thank you for calling Medinah Press Centre." The eruption that followed was like we had scored a late goal in the FA Cup Final, and following a victory circuit of my living room, we dashed off for a Mexican Corona booze up.

The next morning we began the ritual of scouring every national newspaper we could lay our hands on for confirmation, but despite carefully scrutinising every sports page at least half a dozen times, we met with no success. It began to dawn on us that without news of Jay Don Blake's 'Ace' in print, there was a definite possibility that a number of bookies would attempt to withhold payment.

We had for a number of years been subscribing to the popular and very informative American newspaper, 'Golf Weekly'. The in-depth reporting and US tour statistics were a priceless aid in quickly spotting bookmaker ricks in match and group betting, and John thought it would be an idea to ring them to check that confirmation would go in their

U.S. Open review the following week.

After being transferred to the newsroom by a telephonist confused by John's English accent, he began to explain to the now Walter Matthau sounding voice that he was phoning all the way from London, and would the American be kind enough to confirm that Jay Don Blake's 'Ace' would be reported. "Yes, sir," he replied with assurance, "the hole-in-one will definitely be mentioned in the U.S. Open issue out this Wednesday."

John usually found his copy on the doormat about two weeks after publication, but in a state of desperation he explained that he needed a dozen copies urgently. "Sir, the best I can do is to send them out by special airmail first thing Wednesday morning," he replied.

John made his departing thank you, knowing it was Odds On it would probably be at least a ten day job, so other avenues had to be urgently pursued. We decided to drive to Heathrow Airport to try and land the 10,000/1 shot of successfully finding a Saturday edition of the Chicago Tribune complete with details of the U.S Open 'Ace'.

Throughout the journey we also discussed the possibility of one of us flying out to Chicago, because, although that would be quite a drastic move, there were considerable amounts of money at stake. However, our conversation was interrupted by a call on my mobile phone from friend, life long Ben Crenshaw supporter and sports commentator extraordinaire, Angus.

Already conversant with our Hole-in-One activities, he began by congratulating me on 'having it off yet again' but the tone of the conversation soon changed as I began to describe our plight. After listening intently he informed me that he had a very good contact inside the Medinah events centre whom he would ask to arrange for official U.S. G.A. confirmation to be faxed to my home.

I thought all our problems would soon be over and was sure there was now absolutely nothing to worry about, but unknown to me at the time, the real nightmare was about to start.

Bookmakers don't like paying out at the best of times, least of all on the Hole-in-One, especially as they think they are just nicking your stake money when they accept the bet. During the next couple of days spent in the North East the shock of seeing me entering their premises holding a successful voucher had about the same effect as pointing a Crucifix at Count Dracula.

Hull was definitely not one of my favourite places in the world, but with readies to collect, who cares. By mid afternoon on the third day I found myself staring once again at the cartoon Pig and Whistle sign, recalling the bizarre events that had taken place in the public bar just a few days earlier. The betting shop in the car park appeared to be in an even sadder state of decay than before, and with my winning voucher probably being worth more than the entire premises, I thought this could well be another 'keys job'.

The afternoon racing programme was by now well under way, and I decided my game plan was to put just a little more punch into my performance than usual. The manager, busy harpooning chips from a paper bag, appeared to be suddenly overwhelmed as all three punters scrambled to get on the 3.15 race at Pontefract.

"Oh, thank you God - at last," I suddenly shouted out, letting my presence be known. "What a result," I continued looking towards the skies. "What's happened, mate?" he asked looking slightly shaken and not yet recognising the very different me.

"This has really got me out the s**t, man," I went on. "Tell me what the f*!k's happened, mate," he now insisted. The two choruses of "Jay Don Blake, hallelujah!" that followed clearly gave him the right hump. "Who the f*!k's Jay Don Blake?" he now wanted to know.

Already sliding my betting slip under the counter bars, I enthusiastically asked, "Did the governor leave me a kite or is it readies?" The sight of my fourteen fifties prompted the expected but sharp reply, "Nowt on that mate."

"What do you mean?" I asked with a look of shock.

"You heard what I said, there was definitely no hole-in-one. I watched golf on t'telly."

"You're joking," I replied, shoving my bona fide fax confirmation into his hand.

After scanning the type for a few seconds, he blurted, "This means nothing to me mate."

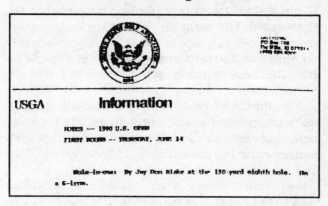

USGA **Information**

NOTES — 1990 U.S. OPEN
FIRST ROUND — THURSDAY, JUNE 14

Hole-in-one: By Jay Don Blake at the 190-yard eighth hole. He a 6-iron.

"Where's the governor, is he in the pub?" I asked. "Gone out," he blurted, adding, "You won't catch him now 'till t'morning." "Look, I just want to be paid on a winning bet," I protested as I began to scratch out about half a dozen sources of definite confirmation on one of the shop's swiped William Hill betting slips, including the phone number of the Golf Weekly newspaper in the US.

"If you can't confirm the result with this lot there's no hope for you, mate," I told him adding, "If the governor wants to phone the States tell him I'll pay the cost of the call out of my winnings." "We've got our own methods of checking," he replied reluctantly accepting the slip.

"Any chance of sorting it out now, then?" I asked. "No chance, mate," came the expected reply, "the governor will want to make his own investigations - after all, it's his money."

"When do I actually get paid then?" I asked. "Call back tomorrow around 2 o'clock, meantime I'll show this to governor round t'pub tonight," he replied, still clutching my fax.

The bookies in Grimsby were giving me a hard time the next morning as I handed out lists of phone numbers and copies of the fax confirmation like confetti, I was mostly resigned to calling back again a week or so later, when hopefully I would have received the Golf Weekly newspapers and confirmation from the Life.

My lunchtime journey across the Humber Bridge back to the Pig and Whistle took little time but the sight of the betting shop manager seemingly sunbathing outside was not at all what I had expected. "I take it there were no problems checking out my best - is the Chief inside?" I asked the manager, who had already departed from the comfort of his garden chair and appearing uncharacteristically cheerful.

"The governor will be here in t'few minutes and he'll sort problem out when he arrives," he eagerly replied.

Thinking the old readies must be on the way from the bank, the few minutes had lengthened into ten, during which time we entered into a little horse-racing banter. With the conversation now running dry, it was becoming apparent the figure coming towards me was the owner, looking something like the long lost brother of Jocky Wilson. He was moving like an unstoppable freight train, and appeared to be on collision course with the shop door. Uttering only a brief "Follow me, son," he brushed past with eyes that refused to acknowledge my presence.

As I entered the empty shop I was within seconds being blasted by the bang of the shop door being slammed behind me. The main source of light had been extinguished, and I heard the sounds of turning keys and bolts. The owner struggled to lock himself in behind the security of his counter: I had been ambushed.

Glaring at me through the security bars he already had the telephone pressed against his ear. I thought he was about to speak to one of his mates with a duffing over being about an Eight On chance, but the arrogant blurting of his first few words quickly put my mind at ease.

"Er, hello, it's Mr. Braithwaite here, can I speak to Detective Inspector Rogers please - that's right, I spoke to him three times earlier this morning." The broad smirk remained as he gloated at his captive. "Er, yes, hello Inspector," he continued, "yes, he's in the shop. You'll be here in about five minutes then."

"That were police," he told me as if I hadn't guessed. "You've tried to f*!+?!g con me, there was no hole-in-one," he went on. "I've been onto local bookies, Habbershaws, phoned golf experts, Surrey Racing, spoke to Ladbrokes and London bookie A.R. Dennis - and all say bet didn't cop."

"Didn't you check out any of the phone numbers I left with the manager?" I asked. "Didn't have to, mate," came the reply, "bet didn't cop." "What about the fax?" I enquired. "That were forgery, you printed that yourself."

I had resigned myself to just sitting down to wait for events to unfold, and shortly the distant sound of police sirens began to get louder, reaching a climax outside the front door. The sound of locks being unbolted was followed by a sudden blast of sunlight as two burly policemen marched in.

Their presence enticed Mr. Braithwaite back out into the shop as they began to listen to the "I've phoned everybody on t'planet and bet didn't cop" routine. Eventually he got round to producing Exhibit A - the alleged forged fax, explaining it contained the Crest of America which in itself was an horrendous offence.

My own vigorous attempt to protest my innocence proving ineffective, I shortly found myself being escorted to the police car which would take me to the local police station for questioning. Forced to endure the manager's idea of a fond farewell, his two fingers slowly faded away as we made our way to the station, where any misunderstanding that had occurred would be sorted out.

Ten minutes of uncomfortable silence spent in the interview room was broken by a welcome appearance by Detective Inspector Rogers. After reluctantly accepting my handshake, all three appeared intent on hearing my explanation in the case, probably the first of its kind in the annals of Humberside police history.

I began my account by describing how I had recently visited all of Hull's bookies and the problems faced by the Jay Don Blake Hole-in-One punters. Fifteen minutes later, engrossed in my story, I was describing in detail Mr. Braithwaite's inefficiency. I concluded by stating I had total confidence in the police, and asked that before they leave to complete the formality of confirming the result, was there any chance of me having a 'Press Up' with any of them.

No longer able to hide their amusement, both Detective Inspector Rogers and one of the policemen left the interview room, only to return just minutes later to break the predicted good news. The companionable detective inspector, at last convinced of my innocence, listened intently as I expressed concern about making yet further attempts to collect my winnings from Mr. Braithwaite.

The offer of a lift in a police car was gratefully accepted, as was his cheery offer to accompany me back to the Braithwaite psychiatric institution. The shifty manager looked as if he had just seen a ghost as we entered, pushing aside the remaining three tassels of the sun blind. Mr. Braithwaite's capture earlier in the afternoon had clearly put him on a high, and he was celebrating by tucking into a large bag of cherries.

My unexpected presence caused his arrogance to change to bewilderment as the Detective Inspector condescendingly broke the news that the police had concluded investigations and were satisfied there had been a Hole-in-One in the U.S. Open, adding that it looked like he would have to pay me out after all.

Looking as if he had just been struck by a bolt of lightning, the stunned silence was broken by the pathetic words, "Well, I apologise to t'lad."

The sweat glands had suddenly been thrown into overdrive as he began to blurt out his list of reliable sources of information explaining that all had told him most decisively, "Bet didn't cop." After three more choruses of, "Well I apologise to t'lad," and then winning the battle to stutter out, "Well, of course I'll pay him." Detective Inspector Rogers tactfully withdrew, signalling that he would wait for me outside.

The reality of having to rake up £750.00 in readies had really blown his brain as the bad tempered ransacking of each of his desk drawers in turn began. The frenzied counting of banknotes that followed led to a hectic rummaging through his pockets, concluding with the ringing sounds of the cash till.

The payment of my winnings was an emotional affair as his shaky hands and nervous twitch went about their task. "Was that a tear rolling down his cheek?" I asked myself as he bravely continued the count until relieved of the full £750.

To conclude, the Detective Inspector asked that before he shot off back to the station, would I be kind enough to answer a few further questions, this time about past 'Hole-in-One' statistics, as he intended to crackaway himself before the next golf tournament ...

11. CHANDLER INSURANCE POLICY

1991.

Sweating out the M25 rush hour crawl from the Dartford Tunnel to a Sandown Park evening meeting is nobody's idea of fun, but arriving late and missing the first winner would certainly put most people off their stride.

"This is Capital Radio Sport and we are going straight over to Angus Loughran for a live report from Royal Birkdale."

"Well, Jeff - the years rolled back today for Lee Trevino in the final practice round of the 120th Open Championship, where he achieved a hole-in-one at the 14th. The roar from the gallery must have been heard in Blackpool. Then, inspired over the back nine, the Mexican finished with a miraculous eagle two on the 18th to record a magnificent 66."

Unfortunately, Trevino's Ace was just in practice: time tunnels not yet being available for the Hole-in-One punters, we could only wish the Open had started 24 hours previously. Although depressing news, missing the EBF Supersloane 2 year old maiden stakes was not going to add to the misery, because finding winners was the last thing on our minds.

The weekly expenses were enormous, but unlike a regular business, we had an angle to offset some of the liabilities - that meant taking out Hole-in-One insurance, but a premium would have to be paid.

The Harpers and Queens Handicap had apparently been an enthralling affair and the bustle of queues collecting winnings was currently taking place. John made for the rails and joined the one man queue at the Victor Chandler Pitch, but when asked for a winning ticket, he then boldly made his request.

"What are the odds for a hole-in-one to happen in the British Open?" he enquired, knowing Victor was already clued up.

"4/6," Victor promptly replied.

"What price is <u>No</u> hole-in-one, then?" asked John despondently, shaking his head but funking a positive response.

"5/4," replied the unflinching bookie.

Victor had laid an Even Three Grand No Hole-in-One way back in the '89 Open and John recalled the relief of at least recovering some of the expenses at that calamitous time.

"If the bet wins, I'll be at Windsor Monday night," was Victor's 'Bon Voyage' as two large was transferred to the Chandler bin. We had guessed if quoting odds reputable bookmaker Victor Chandler would lay a decent bet, and estimated British Open Hole-in-One odds to be around the 1/2 mark. In effect, he had bet 4/5 a Hole-in-One occurring - in our view Victor had the value.

12. A PRAYER ANSWERED

The sun steadily rose through torrents of rain as we headed North up the M6 towards the famous Royal Birkdale Golf Course for Day One of the British Open. The conversation had for some time been about never kipping in the car again as the condensation was still causing aggravation, but it was the approaching unbroken grey skies ahead that were causing much concern.

It's a well known fact that rain and cold causes depression in many - sometimes even suicide, but at the thought of freezing winds racing in from the Irish Sea, creating monsoon conditions. We began to wish our <u>No</u> Hole-in-One bet with Victor had been Twenty Grand.

The whole year's work and investment was in the balance as we reflected on our last big potential payday.

The bookmaking giants had been at the top of the hit list for the '89 campaign with Scotland's Troon venue for the Open Championship targeted for the big one.

Floods of money running on in doubles from the US Open in addition to lumpy bets with bookmakers Brent Walker, Coral's and London's biggest independent Mannings, created a potential £150,000 bumper pay day ... but four agonising days of prayers at the famous 120 yard 'Postage Stamp' hole proved ineffective, as we eventually staggered from the course counting substantial losses.

"Norman will win - what time does Jack Nicklaus tee off?" was the banter on the top deck of free car-park-to-golf-course transportation. These bona fide golf enthusiasts could never have guessed we had wads of Hole-in-One betting slips poised to launch a summer of bookmaker golfing misery.

Play would start at 7.15 a.m. each day with the final three balls departing at around 4.20 p.m. If there were to be a minimum of 1800 attempts at all four par 3's with very strong winds now quickly drying out the coastal greens, our 5/2 estimate only some three hours earlier had now been reduced to British Open statistical Hole-in-One odds of about 1/2 .

The prominent super-heavyweight figure of the Big H appeared to be causing concern amongst the early sprinkling of uppercrust voices and golfing umbrellas as predictably he was silencing every critic. Flamboyant gambler and number one face on the scene for years, he is renowned for having an insatiable appetite for gobbling up anything Odds On.

"F*!k me, when's the last time you bought a new pair of underpants?" the irrepressible figure screamed as, accompanied by entourage, he wobbled over. "You're a f*!+?!g disgrace Bandit, with all the dough you've got," he roared on. "Whey hey, it's the world's greatest splodger," came my response.

I recalled a super confident Big H awaiting the formality of that last selection passing the post to land a

£30,000 long Odds On treble - only to endure a 'marathon sweat up' then throttling for Snooker's Dean Reynolds. "How can you let yourself get done by a Muppet - you're a f*!+?!g class act, Dean," were the Big H's post action screams inside Blackpool's 'Norback Castle' Arena.

"Where d'yar get that jacket from," he then bellowed, now sorting out John. "He's made bundles at the game and comes out wrapped up in his mother's rug," he went on, referring to John's disintegrating tweed jacket, worn 365 days a year since 1981, and now tugging at the Bandit's perishing pants elastic.

"I'd prefer to have Rabies than take a bet off of him," he then screamed out, amidst embarrassed gasps of disapproval.

"All I need to become a multi millionaire is to have two flashing lights fitted to a phone tapping device," he bulldozed on.

"The Red light tells me when the Bandit's having a bet and Green is when Danny Boatman is having one of his two grand straight forecast specials at Romford Dogs!" He turned his attention to the scoreboard.

"'Allo Den, it's the Big H," he was now breathlessly spluttering into a mobile phone.

"I want an Even Ten Grand, D J Russel to beat Brand Snr and a Seven Thousand to Four Eamon Darcy to <u>Do</u> Pinero - that's 18 holes only Den, you got that, <u>only</u> 18 holes," he repeated, staring at a sea of discs beginning the day's journey across the scoreboard.

"They're a f*!+?!g joke this Royal and Ancient - they're not worth that," he now roared, flicking a two pence coin towards the skies. "The world's biggest tournament, and there's no betting allowed," he continued, arms raised, condemning the R & A's strict no-On-Course bookmaker policy.

"That's the kid who cost me Seven Large at Fulford last year," he let it be known to all, pointing towards what appeared to be a conscientious student enjoying some part time employment manning the scoreboard.

"The kid's colour blind," he then screamed, with conviction.

I recalled the erroneous posting of a Red Disc, signifying Peter Fowler to be Two Under Par, that had prompted the Big H to phone through that frantic seven

169

grand bet. Amidst scoreboard confusions, the Big H had
watched in horror as, amended with a Blue Disc, Fowler
was in fact Plus Two.

"I'll bet a million pounds to a carrot he'll f*!k up
the scores before the day's out, Guv," he then bellowed to one of two remaining picnickers about to
depart from the vicinity.

An afternoon of hiking up and down Birkdale's
links on just a couple of hours' kip, and synchro-
nized gut aches caused by either by continuous
Hole-in-One false alarms or the devouring of a
second Hog Roast/Bacon Sandwich/Mars bar treble
had eventually taken their toll. Deciding to make
an early departure, we headed to a hotel in nearby
Wigan.

A chunk was already in the bin following Hole-
in-One success at the first three selected events,
with not only singles but also a substantial number
of doubles having already obliged.

After the weeks of planning, the four months of
six-day weeks dashing round the country's bookies, the excellence of execution in dropping Cluster
Bomb bets not to mention Thirty Grand risked in
stake money - were we ever going to reach that
magical Pot of Gold at the other end of the rainbow? Or to put it another way, would we <u>really</u>
have it off? Tomorrow, with the half way cut looming, was one of the most important days in our
punting careers, but as fate would have it, we did
not have to wait long.

Next Morning

"Please, just for today, give us a hole-in-one, instead of our daily bread!" was the early morning prayer as we peered towards the Lancashire skies, grateful that the Banditmobile had survived the night without a vandalism fine being enforced.

"Ballesteros blows hot" was the headline above the Life's Open report. Regenerated after a good nights kip, we set about scouring a paper each for any Bookmaker ricks before the credit offices opened at 9.30 a.m.

"Surrey racing laid a two grand bet at 7/2," John was reading aloud as I continued my rub down with The Post.

"A streaker tried to embrace Olazabal on the first fairway yesterday," I was then informed, but wondered why his hand had appeared on my shoulder, accompanied by a look that reminded me of Mrs Gonzales winning the T.V. Finals of California's state Lottery.

"Listen to this," he spluttered, barely able to retain his composure. "Brian Marchbank got a hole-in-one."

"What?" replied the Bandit, snatching The Life.

"It must have copped late," yelled the Bandit, rushing back to the hotel reception and buying every paper on the desk to seek confirmation, praying The Life had not made a rick.

We frantically rifled through the papers and soon

struck gold, with the final line in The Telegraph confirming Marchbank's triumph.

> Two incidents enlivened an already lively day. Firstly, the appearance of a streaker trying to embrace Jose-Maria Oalazabal on the first fairway and, secondly, Scot Brian Marchbank producing the shot of the day – a hole in one at the 12th.

The world has seen many emotional moments - Clark Gable ditching Vivien Leigh in the final frames of Gone with the Wind - Charles and Di getting married - Margaret Thatcher leaving No 10, but the ensuing lap of the car park was a scene not witnessed since Hal Irwin's US Open Playoff clinching putt.

"Oh thank you, God," screamed the Bandit in ecstasy. Tears were now rolling down John's cheeks reminding me of Gazza's boat when he was sent off with just five minutes to go in the World Cup semifinal.

"We've cracked it for well over three hundred grand," he continued. "Even the Chandler firms had it off!" he went on, as the Bandit's brain provided some prompt mental arithmetic computations regarding their huge wad of now successful cluster bets.

13. BRITISH OPEN GRAND SLAM

"That European Open must be worth the Crown Jewels to us now," John enthused.

"You two wun t'pools?" the cloth cap jovially enquired as we made our way back to the car.

"What are thee doing wi' t' flower beds?" he then asked, as the Bandit was seen burying his conk deep into Wigan soil.

With John showing all the emotions of a newly crowned Miss World, we set about the day's initial task - to buy out Wigan Town's remaining supply of Telegraphs and Lifes.

The punters of Wigan were definitely not the country's most fanatical as the sixty Telegraphs, compared with just nine Sporting Life's, confirmed. Either paper, complemented with a copy of Marchbanks scorecard, should provide reasonable defence to the predicted:
"Eh? Didnae cop, mates," or "Who's Brian Marchbank?"

Entering PGA Headquarters, keen to get my mitts on 'you know what' before a bite of lunch, I thankfully had few problems. "I guess this is what you're after," I was told by the friendly lady official handing me my copy of the Marchbanks scorecard. She was well aware of my Hole-in-One interests. It was a pleasure to sit on the grass in front of the scoreboard and analyse each player's progress without the stress of waiting for Hole-in-One discs to appear.

The rules of the Royal and Ancient's Open state that the leading 70 players and ties, plus any player within ten shots of the leader, will qualify for the final two rounds. With the cut being made that very evening, it was distressing to recall Surrey Racing's lack of interest in repeating their previous years' generosity when they offered 8/1 two Hole-in-Ones and incredibly 33/1 3 or more.

I was about to take the first bite of my Penguin bar after devouring a £2.80 cheese and pickle sandwich, as the Big H checked up our lunch plans and spent a good ten minutes explaining the urgency of him not missing the mid afternoon flight to Edinburgh to enable him to catch the Powderhall Dog Meeting that evening, assuring us that getting £10,000 on one in the second race would present him with few problems.

Strolling off into the hilly links course the blue over par players were not apparently the day's only casualties. A well-groomed lady spectator, venturing no doubt from the champagne tent without appropriate footwear, was sighted falling arse over tit down one of Birkdale's famous dunes.

Pitching ourselves around the 12th green, our thoughts drifted to the countless bookmakers who had been only too keen to grab our stake money when they thought they were receiving a donation (laying odds of up to 100/1) and who would now be bitterly regretting their generosity.

Within bookmaking circles we were now as notorious as the 'James Gang,' but fortunately for us our efforts were all within the rules of fair play. However, the country's beleaguered bookies would have no doubt enjoyed a good 'hanging' with us as the centre of the entertainment.

The summer of '91 became a misery for the bookies and must have involved endless scenes of panic:

... Boomerangs Racing, accommodating Nigel's willingness to lay John doubles till the cows come home, intended to hedge the lot - but his early morning earner evaporated with William Hills 5/4 quote <u>any named double on the golfing calendar</u>.

... The intensity of Derby's Arthur Whittaker, glued to the Open Golf Radio commentary and praying for no Hole-in-One announcements.

... The South's leading Bookmakers, 'Spectrum,' who had incurred a further £72,000 liability by attempting to recoup their St Mellion loses, were unable to pull the emergency cord with the European Open looming.

Cluster bets were now exploding all over the place - the UK was littered with disaster areas that would stay contaminated longer than 'Chernobyl'.

We were feeling well 'over par' following the previous evening's 'p*?s up' to honour the recently knighted 'Sir Brian Marchbank', as we scoured the leader board searching for clues. A record 113 had survived the cut, but it was Pebble Beach master tactician Mark O'Meara's inspired form, just one shot off the lead, that got us most excited.

Recalling his memorable English Open victory here at Royal Birkdale in '87, we stared in disbelief at Coral's 33/1 offer before the 'horses for courses clue' made our syndicated £200 each way 1/4 1-2-3-4 an absolute nick, and as we skipped to the course on the final morning with adrenalin flowing, O'Meara was now joint leader with the Post's pre Open tip, Ian Baker Finch.

"This is match number 55 ..." the regimental official announced, to riotous applause.

"On the tee, Severiano Ballesteros," he went on, silencing all within earshot.

The crack of the ball, followed by a moderate clapping of hands, meant Seve was now safely on his way.

"He's the only danger to the front two," the Bandit told John as they again analysed the leader board.

- - 4 Baker-Finch, M. O'Meara
- - 3 E. Darly, M. Harwood
- - 2 S. Ballesteros
- - 1 V. Singh, M. Reid

Bogey five gasps from the Gallery were not music to Seve's ears as he trugged to the 2nd tee.

Then ... Ballesteros can be seen walking off the 3rd green in distant silence.

Blimey ... Baker Finch rattles in an 18 footer at the 2nd - he's now the Leader by 1.

S**T ... O'Meara Bogeys the 3rd.

But ... Baker-Finch Birdies the 3rd!

"You've left it miles too late," John breathlessly shrieked as the Bandit frantically dashed across Birkdale's dunes, making for the tented villages mobile phone booth like a scalded cat.

Modern technology provides Bookmakers with instant teletext updates, enabling them to revise odds in play as a golf tournament progresses -

The bygone days of July '84, when Ken Brown's course record equalling 63 at Haggs Castle, with layers being oblivious to early morning proceedings, are long gone. Reassessed at 2/1 with both hands already on the trophy, the bookies were still laying chunks at 25/1 at lunchtime, and to quote Monday's Times, this 'Cost the bookmakers a small fortune'.

Our punting careers, Hole-in-One activities aside, had for some time been in jeopardy, with several bookmakers terminating our credit accounts. In retaliation, we had opened a series of deposit accounts with bookmaking chains while placing Hole-in-One bets using noms de plume.

(Deposit Account - Cash left in branch in return for receipt with Personal Account and Head Office telephone number - bets can be telephoned through up to the sum invested).

Baker-Finch was earlier in the day offered at around the 7/2 mark, but the Bandit was now asking himself "What's Odds On?"

Puffing his way past the scoreboard, clocking yet another Baker-Finch Birdie at the fourth - the greatest start to a final round in Open history - he was soon 'pulling himself up' at the phone booth mumbling, "I'm betting without the favourite."

The Ol' Bandit flicked through his 'William Hill Diary' for a suitable alias.

Northern Outfit, about 20 shops ... No 1, late call contenders ... Previous form they would take a chunk ... Certified long ago as absolute eggs.

The Bandit began dialling ... but all bets had to be telephoned direct to Headquarters.

"Aye say, Devereux here," I was soon telling the voice in my best Prince Charles. "I'm frightfully sorry to bother you," I earnestly continued, "but I want to place a bet on the British Open." Boldly waffling on, trying to sound as if I had just got out of bed.

"I've got the list here, Sir," came the accommodating reply.

"It's 11/4 Ballesteros, 7/2 Baker-Finch, 9/2 O'Meara and 7/1 Harwood," he promptly informed me. I was about to plonk the lot on Baker-Finch, but I had second thoughts as I recalled an 'in running' darts catastrophe some years back.

The ol' Bandit could not believe his luck, with Coral's still offering those early morning 'correct score' odds as the last arrows of the match were leaving the oche ... Backed to win ten grand, that bargain of the year soon backfired, as a telephone call from the distraught racing manager first thing the following morning insisted all bets must be void.

"The match finished at 1.27 and we took your bet at 1.29," I was frantically informed, recalling my dash to the phones.

This painful education told me to moderate the call, and the three hundred quid was accepted thankfully without fuss - but a further phone call to the same mob was an absolute must.

"'Allo, Del 'ere, eh eh, Mr Duffer," I spluttered to the same voice on the egg line. "Ah wanna bet on the Gowf," I continued, smothering any possible Devereux suspicions.

The Del Duffer assault fortunately resulted in the requested bottle at 7/2 being accepted out of a deposited monkey. Feverishly attempting the 'Miss Entwistle' splodge resulted in being bluntly told 'betting was now suspended'. Reflecting on by-gone days of an incredible career of 'in running late calls' - this was one for the Guinness Book of Records.

Eamon Darcy now appeared to the only danger to us copping the O'Meara place money - and what was left of the afternoon was spent cheering him out the frame.

We left Royal Birkdale feeling invincible, as the O'Meara 'sweat up' and Baker-Finch 'nick' had binned us in excess of three grand ... but this paled into insignificance beside the Hole-in-one roller-coaster, which was soon to approach the end of its journey.

The European Open at Surrey's Walton Heath was where we would meet our destiny, and where we would find out whether we had landed 'a decent tickle' or a permanent place in Punting History.

14. 'FALL OUT ZONE'

"The 500 SL is indeed a bargain at £73,999.97 on the road, Sir," the toff salesman assured the Bandit, who was devouring his lunchtime bag of chips.

"A flagship of German engineering," continued the salesman, now eyeballing the C Reg Bandit mobile regarding part exchange.

"One hundred and eight thousand miles is quite excessive for the year," he observed, looking at the mileometer which was now beginning its third lap.

The number of kites and readies stuffed in the hole in one collection bag had encouraged us to consider upgrading our future transportation arrangements: since Monday lunchtime, we had been following a trail of bookies, collecting winnings and slowly making our way towards the Whittaker 'Fall Out Zone' at Derby.

It was 5.45 p.m. as we made for base camp Nottingham with another three grand in the bin. We eagerly discussed the following day's programme - which was to include collecting £15,000 from Derby's 'Arthur Whittaker'.

<u>Wednesday 24th July 1991</u> - <u>Nottingham Post House</u>

Reps exchanged their 'Good Mornings' as we made for the breakfast buffet to make our selections and then search for a pitch. The papers had been late arriving as the Bandit began the day's first rub down with the Sporting Life.

"No black pudding for both of you, Sir," the glum waitress repeated, ignored by the Bandit, who was seemingly hypnotised by the Life.

Bookie hits ace bets out of bounds

WHAT do you think the odds are against there being a hole in one at a major golf tournament?

An unfortunate cashier in a Midlands betting shop thought that it was a 100-1 shot, and laid the bet to £50, three times.

This was a mistake. The little white ball sailed in without having to be asked twice in the Benson and Hedges and Volvo PGA tournaments earlier this year.

And when Brian Marchbank got everything spot-on at the 12th hole on the first day of the Open at Royal Birkdale last Thursday, he completed a disastrous treble for Derby bookmaker Arthur Whitaker.

The punter has not turned up for his £15,000 yet, and when he does, he is going to be disappointed. Arthur doesn't intend to pay.

Yesterday one of the firm's managers said: "We will be paying out but at the correct odds. It was obviously a mistake by an inexperienced cashier. It was an organised operation – I know that the punter also approached another local bookmaker.

Midlands bookmakers don't quite seem to have got the hang of hole-in-one betting. A while ago a gang of punters were said to have cleaned up by persuading small bookmakers to offer fancy prices against aces at the major tournaments.

Holes in one are achieved so often that golf betting specialists Surrey Racing won't even offer odds against them happening and for the Open. Hills were betting odds-on.

Hills spokesman Graham Sharpe said: "People expect long odds but I reckon the true odds are about 6-4.

"It is about 1,000-1 against any decent player getting a hole in one on a par-three hole."

Amazingly, Hills may still be offering over the odds. In 1990, there were holes in one at 30 out of 36 leading tournaments.

A spokesman for Surrey Racing said: "People sometimes go round the country getting odds of 12-1 or even 33-1 from small bookmakers. If I could get 6-1 I would be laughing.

It was the same story from Trevino Bookmakers, one of the few layers advertising prices on a hole in one.

A spokesman said: "We offered 6-5 and didn't do a lot of business but if anyone offered 2-1, I would be backing it myself.

"A few years ago I offered 8-1 and soon realised that it was far too generous."

DAVID ASHFORTH

SPORTING LIFE - July 24th 1991

'Bookie Hits Ace Bets Out of Bounds', was the front page headline. Closer scrutiny revealed that Whittaker was distraught at the prospect of parting with our fifteen grand winnings and didn't intend to pay up.

"A cashier took the bet - We'll pay out only at correct odds," he went on to say.

We read on to our horror that Hole-in-Ones are achieved so often that golf specialists Surrey Racing won't even offer odds.

Whittaker had made his position clear to the world, without speaking to us. However, fearing that his comments might give others ideas, we abandoned the trip to Derby and set about raking in as much dough as possible.

As the day unfolded, switchboards at the Sporting Life became jammed with similar horror stories, although the journey into the Wirral rain and mist concluded with a well pleased John binning bookie Dave Buckly's £1,360 kite to bring the day's total to something over Seven grand. Meanwhile the Derby bookie had been receiving sympathetic phone calls from colleagues across the country.

Thursday 25 July - Haydock Post House

Bookies in the rough

By DAVID ASHFORTH

SMALL bookmakers were busy telephoning the Life yesterday with tales of woe after reading how Midlands bookmaker Arthur Whitaker had been stung by a hole-in-one punter.

One of Whitaker's cashiers had accepted three £50 bets, each at odds of 100-1, against a hole-in-one being achieved at three major golf tournaments, including last week's British Open.

Unfortunately for Whitaker, and for the cashier, all three bets came up.

This was no surprise to professionals for, as the Life reported yesterday, the true odds against a hole in one at a major tournament are less than 2-1.

In 1990, holes-in-one were achieved in no fewer than 30 of the 38 leading tournaments.

The grieving victims include Liverpool's Grandstand Racing.

The three-shop chain accepted two £50 bets at 16-1 for the Volvo PGA and British Open. Another Liverpool shop was offering 18-1.

In nearby Southport, one bookmaker was wishing he had not laid a £50 hole-in-one double while, in Wolverhampton, bookmaker Mike Langley was wishing he had listened to his mother and avoided strangers.

Langley said: "Back in May a stranger with a London accent walked in and asked for prices against a hole-in-one at four major tournaments.

"We gave him 16-1 to four £50 singles. He has won on the Benson and Hedges, the Volvo PGA and the British Open and there is the European Open to come."

When Langley attempted to lay the bets off, the best price he could find was 7-2. "And that", he said, "didn't last for long".

It was a similar horror story in Staffordshire, where Cannock bookmaker Peter Smith took a bet of £200 at 7-1. That was from a stranger, too, giving support to the widely-held view that this was an organised coup.

Meanwhile, back in Derby, Arthur Whitaker was receiving sympathetic phone calls from bookmaker colleagues.

Whitaker has declared his intention of paying out at what he describes as "the correct odds", arguing that his rules require bets of this kind to be approved by the manager.

If a dispute results, Whitaker intends to submit it to the Life's Green Seal service for arbitration.

'Bookies in the Rough' was the Life's headline that morning, as we read that small bookmakers had been busy telephoning the Life with tales of woe after reading how Whittaker had been stung.

They went on to list a number of the grieving victims ... and Whittaker declared his intention to pay out at what he describes as correct odds - and if a dispute resulted, to submit it to the Life's 'Green Seal Service' for arbitration.

Brummie bookie Mike Langley, on the other hand, was apparently wishing he had listened to his mother and avoided strangers - when he attempted to lay off the bets, the best price he could find was 7/2, and that did not last long.

The super shrewd move of leaving cluster bet collections until after the European Open was now in need of urgent review, and as the dining tables were being laid for lunch, we phoned the Life's David Ashforth and made arrangements for a meeting the following Sunday.

Friday 26 July - M6 Southbound

Hole-in-one 'sting' unfolds

By DAVID ASHFORTH

THE extent of the "sting" perpetrated on small bookmakers by hole-in-one punters became apparent yesterday as more bookmakers contacted The Life.

A Cumberland bookmaker who preferred to remain anonymous confessed that he had offered 10-1 against a hole-in-one at the Benson and Hedges tournament, accepted a £50 bet, and then repeated the exercise for the Volvo PGA.

He said: "Two weeks after the first bet the man came in with a photocopy of the successful player's scorecard, and a report from a golf magazine.

"I foolishly laid him the same bet again, and this time he posted me a copy of the scorecard. The postmark was Romford."

Evidence is growing, and it points to a Londoner travelling North and trawling for prices from uninformed bookmakers who think they are realistic but in reality are fatally generous.

Tameside bookmaker Steve Davies remembers a smartly-dressed, well-spoken Londoner arriving at his shop in Greater Manchester and leaving with slips for two £50 bets each at 14-1 against a hole-in-one at the US and British Open championships.

Davies said: "Since then, I have learnt that the same person had been into many other shops in the Manchester area."

The punter has not yet returned for his winnings but, when he does, Davies says that he does not intend to pay him at 14-1.

Yesterday, the Life received a call from a man who claims to have been behind a considerable number of these bets.

"The extent of the 'sting' perpetrated on bookmakers by the hole-in-one punters became apparent yesterday as more bookmakers contacted The

Life", we read that morning as we made our way to Arthur Whittaker's Derby betting shop. The Life went on to say that a Cumberland bookmaker preferring to remain anonymous confessed he had offered 10/1 against a Hole-in-0ne at the Benson and Hedges tournament, accepting a £50 bet, and had then repeated the exercise for the Volvo PGA.

Rumours regarding our identity were adding to the mystery, with reports varying from a lone Londoner travelling North trawling for prices, to an organised gang sweeping the country.

Placing Hole-in-One bets was never an easy task, and called for resilience and nerve, but that was nothing to the bottle needed when collecting winnings. When a bookie has ironed out a chunk - anything is on the cards.

The return to Whittaker had been inevitable, as it was a 'no offers' job that at least one of the three bets placed over three months ago would cop. As John trudged up Stable Street, dabbling with the countless permutations that lay on the other side of Whittaker's door, he felt like he was playing the lead role in 'High Noon'.

We were surprised to see the young beard, having cost Whittaker £15,000, still employed as his representative, and reasoned that the grey head talking on the telephone must be Arthur.

John pretended not to notice the young blood's nudge and whispers as predictably our presence was made known. Discussions on the telephone promptly evaporated as we involved ourselves with a 'Racing Post' pinned to the wall.

"Right, they are in the shop now," could be heard as we focussed our attention on Whittaker.

"That's the end of your little game," he growled, clumsily hoisting himself upright.

"You've had it good for years - but the game's up now," he continued, entering the arena but permitting his supportive colleague on the line to hear more.

"It was a palpable error - look at my rules," he blustered on, directing us to a nicotine stained scroll on the wall.

Whittaker's tactics were to bluff us with a rule relating to bets being verified by the Manager, but this was irrelevant - because if any member of staff accepts a bet at mutually agreed odds it must stand. We found it difficult to swallow his revised ideas of a fair settlement.

"I'm going to settle the Benson & Hedges at 4/5 - that's fair," he scowled. "The Volvo, well that's a bit harder - you can have 5/2," he continued, his flushed features betraying high blood pressure, "and the British Open is about 13/8!"

"100/1 are the odds you laid - you can't make up Mickey Mouse prices and expect us to swallow," John angrily fired back. "It doesn't matter what Ladbrokes', Coral's or Trevino's odds are - you quoted 100/1 and took our money. If all three bets had lost, would you have hunted us down to return our stakes?"

"I wasn't even in the shop," muttered Whittaker, glaring at the embarrassed young beard.

"If you haven't trained your representative correctly, then it is your responsibility," John informed him.

"I asked you to come back when the guvnor was here," mumbled the youngster, putting in his own two penn'orth.

"You said only if I want 'monkey' bets", John fired back, recalling young beard's assurances that odds once laid can't be altered and that all bets accepted came within company limits.

Whittaker, stunned and not even bothering to do the mathematics, grabbed the support of a stool.

"The Life said you would settle by arbitration," I suggested, deliberately softening proceedings.

"I will," was all he could say, snookered by his statement to the Life, and now no doubt wishing he'd kept his mouth shut.

"It wasn't me that grassed to the Press," he then surprisingly snapped, excusing his blabbing that had done our collection campaign few favours.

"I believe you," said John. Whittaker versus the Hole-in-One gang agreed to submit both cases to the Life's Green Seal Service and accept the decision as final, but the very next morning ...

Bookie pays 33-1 'ace'

A NORTHERN independent book-maker who laid 33-1 about a hole-in-one at both the recent Volvo PGA and Open golf championships, said yesterday he had already paid out on the bets and had no intention of doing otherwise, writes Mike Cattermole.

Dave Buckley, who runs just one shop in Ellesmere Port in South Wirral, said yesterday: "If you lay a bet, you have to stick by it and I laid two separate bets of £20 at 33-1 to the same man for a hole-in-one at the Volvo and at the Open. I paid him £1,360 by cheque on Monday.

"We got our fingers burnt but you have to learn by your mistakes and we clearly made a mistake laying 33-1. You have to take your hat off to this man. If the bet had gone down, nothing would have been said, so we

Continued on page 14

RULING ON HOLE-IN-ONE BETS

THE Sporting Life has been asked by bookmak-ers to make a ruling on the hole-in-one issue. Our decision is that there is a world of difference between a palpable error and an error of judg-ment. If a bookmaker (or member of his staff) accepts a bet at mutually agreed odds – and neither the bet nor the laying procedures contravene the bookmaker's rules – there is no way in which the bet can be retrospectively voided or amended.

It is one thing for a bookie's clerk to misread a screen display and for the price to be corrected under a "palpable error" rule, but it is quite another for a bookmaker – who has adjudged that a bet represents a reasonable risk and accepted the business – to attempt to change the terms when his naivete or generosity becomes apparent.

Unless a bookmaker who has laid over-gener-ous odds about a hole-in-one has a clear and unambiguous rule giving him the right to void or amend the bet for good reason, he has no option except to pay up.

Layers at odds over hole-in-one payout

Continued from front page

must take this like men."

It seems Buckley was one of many small northern bookmakers who laid fancy prices about a hole-in-one to what one bookmaker described as a "smartly dressed, well-spoken Londoner".

But unlike Buckley, some bookmakers do not intend to pay out at the prices they laid.

Tony Ambrose, who runs a shop in north Bolton, Lanca-shire, is one who has no intention of settling the bets.

He said yesterday: "This man has done a marvellous job. He had two bets with us of £50 at 25-1, but he hustled us for the price by showing us some old newspaper cuttings about Corals laying him 33-1 a few years ago. It was a mistake on our part to give him the 25-1 and I don't intend to pay out – I can't afford to.

"One of my rules states

that ante-post prices are laid subject to them being correct at the time and, for me, the cashier made an error on the bet. If The Life's Green Seal Service says I have to pay out, then I will delete that service from my rules and abide by my own.

"The day before the Volvo, Trevino bookmakers were offering just 7-4 for a hole-in-one and 5-2 on for no hole-in-one. I will pay out on Tre-vino's price of 7-4 and if the man isn't satisfied, we could negotiate on the price."

Midlands rails bookmaker Don Butler, whose family have been in the business for more than 100 years, added: "No rules have been broken in any shape or form. Basi-cally, the bookmakers had not done their homework. The punter asked for odds that they were not profes-sional enough to handle.

"We can make mistakes and we should pay when we make mistakes. It does the bookmaking fraternity no good to moan about it."

Quit moaning and pay up, bookies are told

by DEREK McGOVERN

BOOKMAKERS who are refusing to pay out on a well-rehearsed golf sting came under fire from a fellow bookie yesterday.

Small independent firms cried foul after a golf shrewdie travelled the country getting fancy prices about holes in one on the bigger European Tour events.

One Manchester firm laid bets of £50 at 14-1 for a hole in one at the Open – even though Corals were offering only 10-11. Now they say they won't cough up.

And a firm in Derby incredibly offered 100-1 for a hole in one in three separate tournaments – and now face a payout of £15,000.

But Alan Jevons, another Manchester-based layer, claims the non-payers are putting the industry in a bad light.

He said: "If these bookmakers offer stupid odds then they must face the consequences.

"This punter has clearly done his homework and got the best prices available. He has done nothing wrong and should be paid out in full."

Jevons said the punter, reportedly a "smartly-dressed Londoner", had visited his shop and asked for a price. "When I offered him 64 he said 'no thanks' and left."

The hard-pressed smaller bookies, perhaps drawing on their own experience on the golf course, have vastly over-priced the likelihood of aces in the big European events.

In 21 European Tour events so far this season there have been 20 holes in one, although six of these came in the Mediterranean Open to Nick at the beginning of the year.

What has hit the bookies particularly hard is the fact that all the big televised European golf events this season have seen a hole in one.

Jay Townsend notched an ace in the Benson and Hedges International, Wrath Grant in the Volvo PGA, Peter Smith in the Murphy's Cup, Eduardo Romero in the Irish Open, Philip Walton in the Scottish Open, and Brian Marchbank in the Open.

When you consider that a normal tournament will offer three or four par-three holes and that about 150 top-notch professional golfers compete in the first two rounds, the majority of them hitting the green, it doesn't take a genius to work out that the odds about a hole in one will be pretty prohibitive.

The hard-hit Derby firm claim a raw casino was hoodwinked by the punter who pretended to be a raw novice, while the Manchester-based firm, who offer to lay any advertised price, claim the shrewdie produced a false leaflet advertising 14-1 for a hole in one at the Open in 1991.

The Derby firm say they will settle at the 'true' odds of 4-1 for the B & H International, 5-2 for the Volvo PGA, and 15-8 for the Open. "Any ante-post bet we lay has to be verified by the manager and the manager was not in when these bets were taken," a spokesman said.

They are not the only victims of the sting. Smaller bookmakers all over the north of England face hefty payouts for a haul which could net the perpetrators anything up to £100,000.

The big firms, who all have specialist golf odds compilers, were left unscathed. Corals spokesman John Wright said: "If these smaller bookies are laying silly prices that's their problem. We get dozens of calls asking for prices about holes in one, most of them from smaller bookmakers. When we tell them something like sevens or 5-4 they are very annoyed. They all think it should be something like 10-1."

"Corals were offering 100-1 about Nick Faldo notching a hole in one at the Open."

RACING POST - Saturday 27 July 1991

Due to unprecedented enquiries to the Life by the country's reeling bookies, the paper decided to print a front page 'ruling' regarding settlement of Hole-in-One bets.

Although totally unexpected, it wasn't a shock that the Life had ruled in our favour, stating:

"There is a world of difference between a palpable error and an error of judgement." They then went on to say:

"It is one thing for a bookie's clerk to misread a screen display and for the price to be corrected under a palpable error rule, but it is quite another for a bookmaker - who has adjudged that a bet represents a reasonable risk and accepted the business - to attempt to change the terms when his naivete or generosity becomes apparent."

This view was upheld by Northern bookie, Dave

Buckley, and numerous other layers, agreeing that once odds had been offered and a bet accepted - that bet, if successful, must be honoured.

The Life's ruling, we assumed, would call the halt to a hard core of non-payers that was beginning to emerge, and as we ended the morning's Egg McMuffin celebrations and headed for an afternoon's racing at Ascot to watch 'Generous' romp home, we both felt on top of the world.

Monday 29 July - 10.30 a.m. - M1 Northbound

The 'Hole-in-One' coup had received front page coverage from the Sporting Life on four consecutive days, and had become a sort of mini-series: today, all eyes were focussed on the back streets of Derby.

The Life's ruling that 'All Bookies must Pay Up' would, we thought at the time, save us the aggravation of writing letters to the Life's 'Green Seal Service.' We were confident that those Arthur Whittaker betting slips would shortly be exchanged for £15,000, but ...

Whittakers, Stables Street, Derby

"Unless a clear and unambiguous rule gives the bookmaker the right to void or amend the bet," again spluttered the whinging Arthur Whittaker, quoting from the final paragraph of the Life ruling.
"Look at this - can't you read?" he furiously continued, one finger seemingly superglued to a rule on the wall. "This states all bets must be

verified by the Manager, and HE is just an office junior," snarled Whittaker, pointing at the disgraced young beard.

"You are a cheapskate!" I erupted in disgust. "If he's in charge of the shop in your absence, he is the Manager," I continued, realising Whittaker was prepared to go all the way to avoid a £15,000 payout. "D'you realise what you've done?" I then angrily yelled, Whittaker choosing to let me have my say. "You've admitted to the Press you are a knocker," I resolutely continued, purposefully eyeballing Whittaker and well pumped up with yet more to say.

"The name Whittaker, once proudly splashed across your shop window, is today in disgrace," I went on, inducing an eerie stillness.

"When Life reports of your whinging are eventually lowered deep into the archives for eternity,

doesn't it worry you that one day in the distant

future a 'Whittaker' studying ye olde Sporting Life's might stumble across his descendants' blackened past?" I persevered to Arthur's horror.

"You're going to go down in history as the Century's most disreputable bookmaker," I solemnly concluded. An uphill struggle still lay ahead if we were to persuade Arthur to part with t'brass.

A shaken Arthur Whittaker had stubbornly rejected the Sporting Life ruling. We left Stable Street having agreed that both sides would submit their accounts in writing to the 'Green Seal' arbitration service - which would be adjudged to be absolute and final.

<u>Tuesday 30 July</u>

The results of Sunday's meeting with Life man David Ashforth appeared in print with the headline. 'Ace punters bunkered in Derby shop' referring to yesterday's Stable Street showdown.

Ace punters bunkered in Derby shop

By DAVID ASHFORTH

THE two punters who have been giving bookmakers nightmares with their hole in one "sting" turned up at Arthur Whittaker's shop in Derby yesterday to claim £15,000.

An employee of Whittaker's laid three £50 bets at odds of 100-1 against a hole in one being achieved at three golf tournaments.

Yesterday Whittaker declined to pay and said he would be submitting the dispute to the Life's Green Seal Service for a ruling.

The two men have spoken to the Life about the operation that could net them over £100,000.

Both in their twenties, they explained: "We are not really gamblers but we went to golf tournaments together and read golf magazines and noticed that there were quite a few holes in one.

"Three years ago Corals offered 16-1 against a hole in one at the Open and 10-1 for the Benson and Hedges.

"They laid substantial bets and paid out and have learnt from their mistake. Now they quote 11-10 on."

A Corals spokesman confirmed this was correct.

Since then the duo have visited "a substantial area of Britain" seeking out attractive odds against aces.

"A lot of bookmakers said

no and a lot said 5-4 - but some offered longer prices.

"It was a gamble that could have gone wrong. There was no guarantee there would be a hole in one.

"Most layers are honourable but others are moaning and groaning, looking for a reason not to pay."

They may be crying again after the US PGA and European Open, on which the terrible two have already placed their bets.

National Association of Bookmakers director Don Butler said yesterday: "At our next meeting I am going to suggest a helpline for new bookmakers. They have not done their homework and will have to pay."

SPORTING LIFE - July 30th 1991

Even the big bookmaking groups, it appeared, were on our side, with Coral's confirming that only three years ago they had offered 16/1 for the British Open and 10/1 for the Benson & Hedges.

The deadly cluster bets had done their work and with the bookies left reeling, Don Butler, Director of the National Association of Bookmakers, was apparently even considering opening up a 'Helpline' for his beleaguered members.

The story had also been picked up by the national press, with the 'Times' quoting Ladbrokes as saying 'It's always tempting to take bets like this, but you really do need the expertise'.

The following day THE SUN reported a similar article:

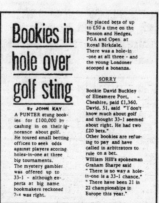

Bookies in hole over golf sting

By JOHN KAY

A PUNTER stung bookies for £100,000 by cashing in on their ignorance about golf.

He toured small betting offices to seek odds against players scoring holes-in-one at three big tournaments.

The mystery gambler was offered up to 33-1 - although experts at big name bookmakers reckoned 7-4 was right.

He placed bets of up to £50 a time on the Benson and Hedges, PGA and Open at Royal Birkdale.

There was a hole-in-one at all three - and the young Londoner scooped a bonanza.

SORRY

Bookie David Buckley of Ellesmere Port, Cheshire, paid £1,360. David, 51, said "I don't know much about golf and thought 33-1 seemed about right. He had two £20 bets."

Other bookies are refusing to pay and have called in arbitrators to rule on a bet.

William Hill's spokesman Graham Sharpe said "There is no way a hole-in-one is a 33-1 chance."

"There have been 21 in 22 championships in Europe this year."

Copping the Crown Jewels appeared to be bang on the cards, as the previous week or so had been spent successfully binning most of the Open Single winnings and doubles. In total, this amounted to about £80,000.

Since the Life's front page ruling a disreputable few, previously named in the press, had stated their intention to settle bets, as in Arthur Whittaker's case, at revised shortened odds.

This group gathered momentum over the last couple of weeks. They seemed intent on waiting to hear the fate of the Derby bookie before paying up.

They were slammed by their peers, as the National Association of Bookmakers released a statement on the 1st August printed in the Sporting Life:

GENEROUS might well have been named after the bookmakers, who took just 6-4 on about him for the King George VI and Queen Elizabeth Diamond Stakes.

But it was incompetence rather than generosity which led those bookmakers to lay 25s and 33s against a hole-in-one at the recent Volvo, PGA and Open golf championships, and the "smartly dressed, well-spoken Londoner" who cleaned up over the bet deserves every penny of his winnings.

The day that any bookmaker lays a bet and seeks to change the odds later when he discovers he has made a mistake in his judgement will be a black day indeed for the profession.

The Bolton bookmaker who was quoted in the Life as saying that, having laid two £50 bets at 25-1 he was prepared to settle them at 7-1, has done little for the trust and confidence upon which betting and bookmaking is built.

To make it worse he went on to say that if The Life's Green Seal Service says he should pay out - which it did - then he will delete that service from his rules and abide by his own.

The big bookmakers would not, of course, have got themselves into this pickle, but had they done so they would have used a different escape route. They would have laid only a tiny part of the bet, as the Coral punter discovered when he could not get more than £25 on a 5-2 chance on which he had wanted to place a £100 at the "guaranteed early morning price."

● Boarderline is contributed on behalf of the National Association of Bookmakers.

Thursday 8th August

'Hole-in-One bets not Void' was the Life's front page headlines as Mike Cattermole wrote:

'The US PGA Championship begins today but there will be no fancy prices offered about a Hole-in-One.' He went on to add, 'The Sporting Life has received numerous letters from bookmakers in the Midlands and North West, caught out by laying over generous prices about Hole-in-Ones.'

Hole-in-one bets not void

By MIKE CATTERMOLE

THE US PGA championship begins today, but there will be no fancy prices offered about a hole in one.'

The Sporting Life has received numerous letters from bookmakers in the Midlands and North West caught out by laying over-generous prices about holes in one

The Life's ruling on the matter was published last month and, so far, in spite of certain protests, in no instances do the bookmakers have reasonable excuses for voiding the bets.

Although the Life will be dealing with each letter individually through its Green Seal Service, the ruling is reproduced here:

"There is a world of difference between a palpable error and an error of judgment. If a bookmaker (or a member of his staff) accepts a bet at mutually agreed odds – and neither the bet nor the laying procedures contravene the bookmaker's rules – there is no way in which the bet can be retrospectively voided or amended.

"It is one thing for a book-ies' clerk to misread a screen display and for the price to be corrected under a "palpable error" rule, but it is quite another for a bookmaker who has adjudged that a bet represents a reasonable risk and accepted the business to attempt to change the terms when his naivete or generosity becomes apparent.

"Unless a bookmaker who has laid over-generous odds about a hole in one has a clear and unambiguous rule giving him the right to void or amend the bet for good reason, he has no option except to pay up."

Derby bookmaker Arthur Whittaker laid £100 at 50-1 three times for a hole in one at the Benson and Hedges, the Volvo PGA and Open Championship.

When Brian Marchbank got a hole in one at Royal Birkdale, it completed a disastrous treble for Whittaker.

Holes in one at the top championships are achieved so often, golf betting specialists Surrey Racing don't even offer a price on them.

They went to to reproduce the ruling with the Life's word on the Hole-in-One issue being a resounding 'all bookies must pay up'.

Wednesday 21st August

The Life arbitration regarding Arthur Whittaker arrived that morning, and to our great relief ruled that there was nothing in his rules to release him from his obligation to pay out on the bets in full.

We did not waste much time, returning to Derby's Stable Street. Only a £15,000 kite would save Arthur from the Almighty.

The hectic goings-on surrounding the distraught Arthur Whittaker made me fantasize about what it must have been like during the final few hours in Hitler's bunker, as an unfamiliar face intently tapped away on a calculator, with young beard taking care of some jottings.

"So there's only four and a half grand in the Abbey," we were sure we heard the moody Arthur say before he became aware of our presence. He irritably waffled his reasons for the post dating of our cheque, and the presentation speech concluded with us being told we were being barred from all Arthur Whittaker premises for life.

The days that followed were spent collecting a further £25,000 from the band of whingers that had regarded Whittaker as a sort of Test Case - their leader had fallen and now, reluctantly, most of them paid out.

15. A DATE WITH DESTINY

Thursday 22nd August

Deadly duo sweat on Euro ace

THE full extent of the hole-in-one betting coup masterminded by two young men from Essex was revealed yesterday – and it is not over yet, writes DAVID ASHFORTH.

The deadly duo, who have been travelling the country breaking bookmakers' hearts with a string of successful hole-in-one golf bets, stand to win a staggering half a million pounds if someone scores an "ace" during next week's European Open golf tournament at Walton Heath.

Holes in one by Jay Townsend at the Benson and Hedges Open in April, by Wraith Grant in the Volvo PGA Championship in May and by Brian Marchbank in the British Open last month have already netted the pair £300,000.

The European Open is the second leg in a series of double bets struck by the punters and success at Walton Heath will add another £200,000 to their bulging coffers.

It has now emerged that well over 50 bookmakers have lost out to the punting partnership, who have taken full advantage of over-generous odds

Continued on page two

DON'T MISS THE SPORTING LIFE WEEKENDER – OUT TODAY

Deadly duo

Continued from front page

offered against a hole in one at a number of major tournaments.

Many bookmakers were under the impression that the bet was a genuine long-shot. In practice, holes in one are commonplace and realistic odds against the eventuality would be nearer to even money than the 10-1 or more laid by many unwitting bookmakers.

Arthur Whittaker of Derby actually laid three £50 bets at 100-1 and on Tuesday the winning punters banked a cheque for £15,000 from Whittaker after the Sporting Life's Green Seal service had ruled in their favour.

Whittaker is not the only layer to have offered 100-1.

Yesterday the two men said: "A bookmaker in Manchester and another one in Nottingham both laid bets of £50 at 100-1 and have paid out with a smile.

"Most bookmakers are reputable and have now paid us – but some have not and these cases are being arbitrated by your Green Seal service."

The men emphasised that there was absolutely no certainty that the bets would prove to be winning ones, and recalled that an attempt to win £150,000 at the 1989 Open at Troon came unstuck.

They said: "Three of the par three holes were the longest that you have ever seen and the fourth was the famous Postage Stamp hole. We stood there praying for four days but it was no good."

The pair have not confined their efforts to Britain. Last year they visited Australia in search of odds against a hole in one at the Australian Open.

There was a hole in one but unfortunately no one prepared to offer odds against it.

They have also been to Ireland and to the USA and that is where they plan to holiday next year.

One of the men said: "We will take a month off and visit Gulfstream Park in Florida. I want to sit by the paddock and think of something new."

That could spell trouble for Britain's beleaguered bookmakers.

'The full extent of the Hole-in-One betting coup masterminded by two young men from Essex was revealed yesterday - and it is not over yet,' wrote David Ashforth.

'The bookmaking world was further rocked by

revelations that the Duo would land a staggering £1/2 million coup if in two weeks' time an Ace was scored in the European Open at Surrey's Walton Heath.'

Bookmaker disreputability being a subject close to our hearts, and having suffered at the hands of the unscrupulous, we could not resist an opportunity to cause the biggest splash since Watergate.

Hole-in-one punters call for new bookies' charter

By DAVID ASHFORTH

ALL off-course layers should be required to lodge their rules and any amendments to them with a governing body, and prior notice should be given of forthcoming changes in a bookmaker's rules.

That is the view of the two punters behind the hole-in-one coup.

They explained yesterday: "There is a hard core of bookmakers who will try anything to get out of paying.

"When we have gone to

claim our winnings, these bookmakers have pointed to rules that are completely irrelevant."

In some cases, the duo believe that new rules have been invented and displayed, sometimes handwritten, to enable a bookmaker to refuse payment or to impose punitive limits.

Responding to the suggestion, BOLA's director general Tom Kelly said: "It is difficult to know what the

body would be and the law does not allow us to enforce bookmakers rules.

"We have never had a complaint of a rule being changed after a bet has been laid and I don't believe that it happens to any extent.

"On the whole the betting public finds the existing arrangements satisfactory, and if there is a problem punters can approach the Life's Green Seal service or have recourse to Tattersalls Committee or object to the bookmaker's permit."

Race by race punters provide little threat to bookmakers. While employed for 10 years as Manager for one of the leading multiples, John recalls just two shop payouts exceeding ten grand - it is no surprise therefore that late rule changes rarely make the headlines.

Success with the Hole-in-One coup led to us collecting chunks from the bookies nationwide ... but our experiences were to make nonsense of Mr Kelly's assumptions.

Thursday 29th August - Day One - European

Open

Inside the Pro's Shop:

"I'd bet myself at Evens to collect four times out of five playing with these," boasted the Bandit swinging a ping zing 4 iron, intending to play every golf course in Southern Florida during the winter months. Convalescence was badly needed, because the excitment of setting up the chance to Get Out for Life and the stress - caused mainly by recent bookmaker aggravation - had led to many sleepless nights for the Bandit, and he had again found himself in his doctor's surgery.

"Aren't these what Neil Foulds takes?" he had asked his GP, who was prescribing tablets to slow down the Bandit's heart rate - but Hole-in-One anticipations tend to render the weaker sedatives useless.

The European Open was last held at Walton Heath in 1989 in near perfect weather conditions. With that year's Hole-in-One form as a further guide (N Faldo practice, M Allen U S Tournament) we estimated no bigger than a Bottle On chance of the bet copping again at the Surrey course.

Bermuda shorts of varying shades of yellow, and matching shirt, complemented by red braces, was the Big H's choice of attire. Flushed with rage, it was clear a very dangerous 'Dog' was on the loose.
"I'm too big for everyone," he was boasting, angered that on course bookmaker William Hill had declined his Two Grand Jeff Hawkes three ball

request. "Minimum trebles because it's P G A rules is b!?*?+ks," he continued his complaint.

"South African bookies would be shot if they pulled a stroke like this," I was then told, as Big H recalled a drama during last winter's vacation.

"I went through Turffontein turnstyles with my pockets on the deck - Forty Grand in Rands is a lot of dough, Bandit," he went on. "anyway, I got the nod for a good thing in the 4th race, and needed police protection then oxygen after dragging two suitcases to a taxi. Even playing away from home the Big H can't be beat but I got f*!?*d with South African exchange rates and ended up walking through customs with Rands stuffed up my sleeves," Big H reminised ruefully. "If I hadn't come back I could have lived like Kerry Packer for the next 300 years," he concluded.

Sadly, by mid afternoon I was consuming my seventh chilli topped jacket potato and realised my nervous eating problem was once again completely out of control.

Three hours of prayer glued to the scoreboard had yielded a light sprinkling of yellow discs, but as they signified worthless Eagle Threes, they were nothing more than Fools' Gold.

I dared not contemplate my potential mental state if I were still pitched here on Sunday. In search of therapy, I recalled the final round of the '89 Benson and Hedges at Fulford, when wandering in the dusk with all hope gone, we were ignited by Steen Tinning's miracle into jubilant celebrations amongst the cow pats.

Natural instincts to suss out the winner had been disregarded, but with Australian Mike Harwood making a charge we ventured to the action. The greens' undulations were being meticulously studied by both player and caddy, who concluded that the break would be a shade to the right.

"He's got this fifteen footer for a Birdie," whispered a voice, as Harwood prepared for that crucial lead-clinching putt. Punter's Club member 'the Hunch,' whose presence had been noted nearby, appeared to be in a state of distress, frantically poking the buttons on his mobile phone.

Harwood's final backswing was now in motion and the gallery observed a hushed silence.

" 'Allo. Is that Victor Chandler?" came the loud and intrusive sound of 'The Hunch' as he shouted into his phone. "Is Harwood still 40/1?"

Everyone turned and glared at him. Cold stares of disgust meant disgrace for 'The Hunch' and his prompt departure was an absolute must.

Harwood had just about recovered his composure when a deafening roar could be heard in the background - what did it mean?

The blast of spectator noise suggested a possible Faldo Eagle Three, or more likely a Ballesteros chip in, but it came from the vicinity of the seventh green - a Par 3!

A dash to the scoreboard was now underway, but my thumping heart and a stitch meant I had soon run out of puff. A breather and a pee brought much relief but were dreams to become reality? Had the hard work paid off?

A Mercedes 500 SL ... no mortgage ... no 9 - 5 job ... winters spent sunbathing at Florida's Gulfstream Park Racecourse, thinking up another master coup.

The shimmering mirage was at long last a possibility. Had we landed the Big One? It was to be the Big H who would provide the first clue.

"I know golf's your game, but no one can touch the 'Dog' at snooker," he screamed, as we clocked match number 30. "Jiminez got a hole-in-one at the seventeenth and won himself a watch," the baseball hat confirmed.

Is Beadle about? ... he can't be ... he wasn't ...

"Oh thankyou, strange powers," screamed the Bandit, shaking with elation.

"There's only us two left in the game, Bandit," the Big H then had to confess, but knew I wasn't, and never would be, a rival to the country's biggest splodger.

"Another yellow disk, sir," began the champagne cheers and seafood celebrations that were to conclude one of the biggest and most successful coups in gambling history.

Spanish golfer, Miguel Angel Jimenez, with his 6 iron shot at the 17th hole, had earned us at least half a million pounds. That worked out at about £3000 a yard.

6 iron ·GA EUROPEAN OPEN
WALTON HEATH GOLF CLUB

29th, 30th, 31st August and 1st September 1991

Match: 30
29 AUG 91
·Miguel Angel JIMENEZ Sp

Time: 12.05
Round: 1

Tee: 1 73.

Marker's own Score	Hole	Yards	Par	Comp. Score	Hole	Yards	Par	Comp. Score	Marker's own Score
5	1	442	4	4	10	343	4	3	4
6	2	521	5	5	11	528	5	5	6
4	3	391	4	4	12	456	4	5	5
5	4	427	4	3	13	466	4	5	5
3	5	174	3	4	14	465	4	5	6
6	6	494	5	6	15	408	4	3	4
4	7	400	4	5	16	475	4	4	4
4	8	399	4	4	17	155	3	1	3
4	9	189	3	3	18	430	4	4	
	OUT	3474	36	38	IN	3726	36	35	
					OUT	3437	36	38	
					TOTAL	7163	72	73	

MARKER'S SIGNATURE

COMPETITOR'S SIGNATURE

John had a chilled bottle of vintage champagne ready to present to the Spanish hero, but unfortunately he was nowhere to be found.

The past failures of Troon and Melbourne were distant memories, as the reality of our dream coming true had proved how much can be accomplished if totally committed to achieving a goal.

But it didn't stop there ...

16. TABLOID SUPPORT

With all eyes anxiously focussed on Walton Heath, it was no surprise that the Life's next morning front page headline was:

Ace sinks bookies for £½m

THE two Essex hole-in-one punters who stood to complete a £500,000 betting coup if there was an ace in the European Open did not have to wait long to collect, writes JEREMY CHAPMAN.

Spanish golfer Miguel Angel Jimenez holed out with a six-iron at the 155-yard 17th hole during yesterday's first round at Walton Heath.

He won himself a gold watch and might well be in line for a nice drink or two from the intrepid "ace" punters who have sent small bookmakers, especially in the Midlands, reeling.

Jimenez's feat meant that the deadly duo have added another £200,000 to the £300,000 they had already won.

The European Open was the second leg in a series of doubles which have netted the pair the biggest golf killing of all time.

Already Jay Townsend in the Benson and Hedges International at St Mellion in April, Wraith Grant in the Volvo PGA Championship at Wentworth in May, and Brian Marchbank in last month's Open Championship at Birkdale had holed in one to send dozens of bookies into a flat spin.

Derby bookmaker Arthur Whittaker even involved The Sporting Life's Green Seal Service in adjudicating whether he must pay out on three £50 bets struck at 100-1. The Life ruled the bets perfectly legitimate. Eventually Mr Whittaker stumped up. Others paid up without a whimper.

The true odds are not much more than even money. This year, there have been even more holes in one than normal. The European Open is the 27th tour event of 1991 and there have been aces in 15 of them.

The full extent of the coup is still not completely known. Bookmakers all over the land are still ringing The Life for advice. Altogether it would appear that well over 50 small firms have laid – and paid – on vouchers from 10-1 to 100-1.

One thing is certain, next year the two clever punters will have to think up a new money-making scheme now they have finally been rumbled.

'The two Essex Hole-in-One punters who stood to complete a £500,000 betting coup if there was an ace in the European Open did not have to wait long to collect', wrote Jeremy Chapman. 'Spanish Golfer, Miguel Angel Jimenez, holed out with a six-iron at the155 yard 17th hole during yesterdays first round at Walton Heath.'

Chapman concluded:

'The full extent of the coup is still not completely known. Bookmakers all over the land are still ringing the Life for advice. Altogether it would appear that well over 50 small firms have laid - and paid -

on vouchers from 10/1 to 100/1. One thing is certain, next year the two clever punters will have to think up a new money-making wheeze now they have finally been rumbled.'

Friday 30th August 1991

THE SUN'S FRONT PAGE HEADLINES

'Two mystery punters caned bookies for £500,000 yesterday after a golfer scored a Hole-in-One.

The gamblers, in their mid-20's, placed single and double bets linking the European Open with three earlier championships, and yesterday Miguel Angel Jiminez hit an Ace on day one of the championship at Walton Heath, Surrey.

Miguel Jimenez took the Essex duo's winnings to more than £500,000 from an outlay of about £7,500, quite legally.

But giant William Hill was not hit, a spokesman said. "We do our homework - There have been 21 Holes in One in 22 championships in Europe this year - A Hole in One at the European Open is virtually odds-on."'

SUNDAY LUNCHTIME, 1st September, The Bandit Residence

With the aid of a go-between, the Sun's John Kay enthusiastically informed us that we were the toast of the Wapping Office, and offered us the chance of an Exclusive to reveal our mindblowing details of the coup.

TUESDAY 3 SEPTEMBER

Coup what a scorcher! John, left, and Paul, in masks to protect their identity

'HOW WE TOOK BOOKIES FOR £500,000 BY THE HOLE-IN-ONE GANG' read the Sun headline.

The Hole-in-One Gang yesterday revealed the secrets of how they caned the bookies in a £500,000 sting betting on golf.

The two men who pulled off <u>One of the Biggest Coups in Gambling History,</u> said "It was all down to homework and phenomenal hard work." John Kay went on to report: "In a complex operation planned with military precision the duo:

* Got hold of 50 copies of Yellow Pages spanning the country.

* Combed through the directories using marketing pens to highlight one man betting shops and small chains.

* Bought maps for the whole of Britain and worked out routes to take in a target of up to 35 shops a day.

* Drove 212,000 miles in four years as they crisscrossed Britain placing small bets.

* Stayed in the best hotels so they would be 'mentally fresh'.

* Started work at 10.15 a.m. when most bookies open, not stopping until they closed.

* Kept a large filing cabinet of addresses, maps

and betting slips.

For 1991, they selected five tournaments to bet on - the Benson and Hedges, the Volvo PGA and the Open in Brtain, plus the US Open and the European Open.

A total of £30,000 was staked in a series of single and double bets on Holes- in-One at the five tournaments.

Aces were recorded in all five - the last in the European Open at Walton Health, Surrey, last week.

When it was struck by Spaniard, Miguel Angel Jimenez, it took their total winnings past £500,000 - <u>all of it perfectly legal</u>.

The lads were at the tournament and tried to buy Jimenez a bottle of champagne but could not find him.

Paul said, "All we can say is thanks very much Miguel."

Our story proved so sensational it even knocked the Page Three girl onto Page Five but it wasn't over yet ...

"I'll never let those two sting me again," fumed Whittaker. "I felt like getting disinfected after I handed over the cheque - I just wanted rid of them as soon as possible - I could not believe it when the Sporting Life ruled in their favour."

Whittaker, who runs two shops in Derby, said, "Four years ago I quoted them 8/1 against a Hole-in-One. It didn't come off and they came back the next year - I refused to take the bet and if I had been in the shop this time I would have told them to**** off, I never want them in my shop again."

John said in response,

"When I went to collect the cheque Mr Whittaker did not look very happy. Some bookies didn't want to pay out at first and resorted to the rules to try to wriggle out - but others behaved very honourably and some actually congratulated us."

<u>Saturday 7th September</u>

The controversy raged on as Arthur Whittaker's remarkable outburst in the Sun infuriated Channel 4's Racing Pundit, John McCririck, as he wrote in

Derby bookie Arthur Whittaker, stung by the hole-in-one gang, was still seething last night after paying out £15,000 to the ace duo.

Whittaker, 55, fumed: "I felt like getting disinfected after I handed over the cheque. I just wanted rid of them as soon as possible."

The bookie tried to get the wager declared void on the grounds that his shop rules stated all advance bets must be verified by the manager.

He said: "I was not in the shop at the time and one of my junior assistants took the bet, so it was not verified.

"I could not believe it when The Sporting Life ruled in their favour"

Whittaker, who runs two shops in Derby, said: "Four

years ago I quoted them 8-1 against a hole-in-one. It didn't come off and they came back the next year.

"I refused to take the bet. And if I had been in the shop this time, I would have told them to **** off.

"I never want them in my shops again."

But bookie David Buckley, who paid out £1,360, said: "I take my hat off to these guys. They did their homework and we didn't."

Buckley, 51, who runs a shop in Ellesmere Port, Cheshire, said: "When I offer a price, I stick by it. I don't start crying when punters win."

209

his weekly 'At Large' column in the Racing Post.

The coup captured the public's imagination and within days the story was relayed around the Globe.

Punters making killing on holes-in-one

Star Foreign Service

LONDON – South African bookmakers are warned steer clear of two punters named John and Paul placing huge bets on holes-in-one

For the close pals have just cleaned up British bookmakers to the tune of about R12.5 million in a massive series of bets on golfing aces at five major tournaments. And now they're hinting that they are looking for new hunting grounds, including Las Vegas, South Africa and Australia.

The duo, who are understandably reluctant to further identify themselves, say they have done nothing illegal. They have simply exploited bookmakers' ignorance of golf.

They criss-crossed Britain placing bets at odds ranging from 10-1 to 100-1 on holes-in-one being achieved at the Benson and Hedges, the Volvo PGA, the British Open, the US Open and the European Open.

Both previously worked as betting shop managers and decided to exploit bookies' ignorance of golf. Many of the smaller operators, they said, did not realise that holes-in-one were recorded at just about all major tournaments.

Now they are planning to write a book about their venture.

(Johannesburg Star).

and with further credits of:

"Golfing Heroes"   (Odds On Magazine)

Brian Marchbank

GOLFING HEROES

One of the most cheering bits of news for punters this summer was the hole-in-one sting, reported by David Ashforth in the Sporting Life.

If quizzed on the subject, most of us would probably give fairly hefty odds against a hole-in-one happening at any given tournament, which is exactly what bookmakers from all over the country did, at prices from 14-1 up to 100-1.

However, as a couple of smart operators discovered, the odds are very much shorter than that. In fact, according to the Life, they are "much less than 2-1" – and judging by 1990 when it happened 30 times out of the 38 leading tournaments it is more likely to be nearer 1-2.

The two punters, both in their twenties, toured the country placing bets to net themselves over £300,000. Most bookmakers accepted the sting and put it down to experience, but a couple declared they wouldn't pay out.

Happily the Life judged that save for specific instances of "palpable error" the bets should be settled.

If there is a hole-in-one at the European Open, which started yesterday, they will win a further £200,000, bringing their winnings to £1/2-million!

So it's congratulations to the wiley pair – if they'd care to contact us we would love to do a feature on them!

210

FROM THE RAILS
Stories of hyphens and aces

By JEREMY CHAPMAN

Trevino is the one bookmaker which advertises odds against a hole-in-one. It has been 7-4, but for the Open they went 6-3. If you thought there would be no hole-in-one, you could back your judgment at 8-13. Brian Marchbank's first-day ace at the 12th was the 20th of the season, so 6-5 was by no means unfair.

However, stories subsequently filtered through that unsuspecting little one-shop bookmakers in the Midlands and the North had been laying up to 100-1 to well-dressed strangers with a London accent. Not me, sir.

People who don't play or follow golf seem to believe that aces happen only once in a blue moon and then only by some fluke. How else can you explain why Derby bookmaker Arthur Whitaker laid 100-1 against aces in the Benson & Hedges, Volvo PGA and the Open? The punter, who had clearly tried this little game before, had £30 on each. The bookmaker is now squealing that it was an error by an inexperienced cashier, that he's been "had", and that he won't cough up the £15,000 winnings. Instead, he intends to settle at the "correct odds".

Of course, it was an organised operation. Of course, it's been going on for years. A team of 'ace' punters have been sweet-talking small bookmakers into laying them 10-1, 14-1, 20-1, 33-1 and now, it seems 100-1. In Liverpool, three £50 ace bets were struck at 16-1 and 18-1 on the Open.

Back in May a stranger walked into Wolverhampton bookie Mike Langley's shop and managed to obtain four £50 bets at 16-1 against holes-in-one at the B & H, the PGA, the Open and the European Open. So far the first three have all come up trumps. What bad luck he didn't back the accumulator! At Cannock, in Staffs, bookmaker Peter Smith got lumbered with a £200 bet at 7-1, again from a stranger to the town.

But there's nothing illegal about it. Betting, and obtaining the best odds, is a battle of wits. Usually, the odds favour the bookmaker. That's why he takes his holidays in Antigua or Bermuda while the poor mug punter has to settle for Clacton or Blackpool.

Occasionally, the bookmaker makes a mistake and the punter gets a bargain. I hope that, by the time this article appears, Mr Whitaker, far from trying to get out of his £15,000 commitment, will have paid up like a man. After all, with Trevino regularly advertising hole-in-one odds in the trade press, there can be no excuse for the small man who does not know his subject. ●

We found ourselves appearing on BBC Radio's 4s 'Midweek' programme as celebrities.

17. POT OF GOLD

With a caseful of street maps, betting slips and itinerary sheets, and a certain sense of urgency, we headed northwards to embark on the £$^1/_2$ million hole-in-one round up.

The first destination of the three week collection campaign was to be the East Midlands ... Birmingham and the surrounding districts;

... Shamrock Racing pays £32,000 and now quotes a miserable 4/9 for any major golf tournament in 1992.

... Pattersons T/A, the doubles and Yankee bet come to £25,000, but we swallow when the shop's £20,000 limit is imposed.

... Boomerang Racing's Nigel regrets consulting his club pro about Hole in One odds, and stumps up £30,000.

... The Guvnor of the Sports Investments Group will never again leave his son in charge of the business, and coughs up £25,000.

... Terry Turner pays out £13,600 and will always thoroughly scrutinise strangers' bets in future.

Throughout gambling history, there can rarely have been a bet devised that could transform the friendly smiles of accommodating bookies to such drastic effect that, on occasions, collecting winnings was more like taking part in an episode of "Tales of the Unexpected".

Collecting winnings had always been a stressful task, but when the next bookie promptly offered congratulations, insisting on vigorously shaking the Bandit's hand, the pressure appeared to be off.

"Here's your fifteen hundred quid," I was assured, as a wad of bank notes was produced from his herringbone jacket pocket.

"You must have really had it off," he continued, but when he then surprisingly asked for a quiet word outside, my stomach began to roll.

"I knew you'd done me about five minutes after you left the shop," he purposefully informed me.

"I phoned round and was only quoted 10/11 by Coral's," he continued.

"You really put me in the s**t because everyone round here was trying to bail out themselves," he went on.

"You've taken it well, though," came my reply hopefully offering some consolation.

"As it happens, you finished up doing me a bit of a favour," he then chuckled.

"I took the wife up to Newcastle to see her mother

a couple of weeks before the British Open, and spent an evening at a local dog track. Nobody knew me up there so I decided to chance my luck with your bet, but I wasn't able to pluck up the courage to ask until after the fourth race," he went on, with a gleam in his eye.

"What happened?" I asked with genuine interest.

"I got on and averaged about 20/1 to my money - there was no point in being greedy, so I just went down the line betting in fifteen quids and by the time I'd finished I stood to win a couple of grand."

"What a result!" I remarked, intent on hearing more.

He went on:"My hole-in-one bets had rapidly become the evening's main topic of conversation, but as the mumblings and cold stares intensified my sense of unease, I abandoned the meeting as the hare was running for the sixth race," he explained with a twinkle of amusement.

"Did you get paid all right?" I asked, rating it a twenty on chance that he had.

"I waited until the meeting was well under way before I began collecting, only to be unanimously accused of conning the lot of them," he replied in anguish.

"Getting paid out is never a picnic," I assured him, recalling the pain caused by knockers. "They all coughed up - what else could they do?" he naively blurted. Blitzing the country made it inevitable that someone with initiative would sooner or later venture to become a fellow prospector, but most bookies would have been too busy arranging "late entries to their rules" to have even contemplated such enterprise.

September 16th 1991

Early Evening, Lancaster Post House Hotel

An evening scattering of sales rep suits and ties at reception made leather bound briefcases about the only thing we had in common. 'A week at the office' for us had meant collecting cash and cheques totalling £175,000 from East Midlands Bookies.

Tuesday 17th September

Phase two of the collection campaign saw the Banditmobile darting through the back street jungles of Manchester and Liverpool, eventually working Northwards to the Cumbrian countryside. We were ahead of schedule and up to speed, but all was not plain sailing.

... after four days of 'Please call back,' a Bolton bookie painfully parts with £7,500.

... 'Pheasant's orf the menu for good,' as Stafford hands over £8,200.

... After questioning the validity of a Liverpool bookie's limits the Guvnor is summoned to the premises - accompanied by gorillas. The Bandit is soon persuaded that £5,000 is better than being 're-arranged'.

... The Doug Compton Bookmaking chain who "wouldn't have cared about paying out to a local punter, but it had to be bloody southerners" - chokes up £16,000.

... A Manchester bookie irons out £10,000 but punishes his manager's odds-compiling skills by making him pay half from his wages. When he tearfully tells the Bandit he is getting married the following week, reduced winnings of £7,000 are binned.

... The Scotsman's successor insists that his Company remain anonymous as £20,000 is handed over.

Good fortune stayed with us as we completed the North West round up before setting off for an out-of-town bookie, which until now had been left on hold due to its financial insignificance.

Our deluxe edition road atlas displayed a microscopic red line worming its way through a green mass before identifying the isolated town of 'Oakthorne'.

It took about fifty minutes of muddy 'C' road driving before the distant church steeple stirred the Bandit's memory of the town's bookie - victim of Fourteen score.

The decaying frontage was doing little for the

ambience of the surrounding 18th century buildings, but a message scribbled on scrap paper pinned to the door said "bookie can be found in Labour Club." Followed by some local guidance, this led me to the hustle of a bar where the familiar belly, now sporting a shrunken Lancs cricket jumper was waddling towards a one armed bandit, seemingly intent on ironing out some shop takings.

"Sorry to drive you mad," I said cheerfully, but my enthusiasm soon dampened as he chose to ignore my presence.

"You must remember me, I'm the golf bet man," I persisted, as he began feeding the seven melons fruit machine.

"I hope you don't mind me bothering you."

"I was wondering when you'd turn up," he arrogantly interrupted, thumping the nudge button.

"What's all this about? I've had a straightforward bet, and I want to be paid," I protested, resigned to aggro.

"My rules say if a bet's taken in error I don't have to pay out," came his whinging excuse.

"How on earth can a bet be taken in error if you've offered odds and accepted the bet yourself?" I angrily protested.

"All bookmakers have rules to protect them from tricksters like you," came his pathetic response.

"Where's my three hundred quid winnings?" I pleaded.

"I'll get you a drink," he then surprisingly insisted, scrambling for the bar. "I'm a fair man and a sportsman," he slobbered, handing me my orange juice.

"Now I'll tell you what I'm prepared to do," he went on, laying five twenty pound notes on the bar. "You say I owe three hundred quid, and I say you get nowt," he then spluttered.

"What is all this? I just want to be paid," I protested.

"I'll toss you for the hundred quid - that's all you're getting, lad," he told me revealing his scheming hand.

"You get cash on t'counter if you win, and nowt if you lose - a bloody good deal for a con bet," he continued, producing a ten pence coin.

Confronted by yet another mugger masquerading as a bookie, any suggestion of a Life arbitration appeared about as pointless as asking Mecca to re-open my credit account.

"Jack, you're needed as referee," he bellowed to the Landlord as arriving spectators jostled for a pitch.

Playing away from home, and eager never to return to an atmosphere which was as frenzied as an Aussie pub where the sheep shearers playing 'two-up' bet their entire month's earnings on the toss of a coin, I resigned myself to being stitched up.

Amidst the jeers the spun coin led to a scramble as the referee now declared the table area temporarily off bounds.

"That's fair - that's fair," spluttered the bookie, as Her Majesty's head was now officially confirmed by the referee.

Relieved at salvaging at least something, I chose to ignore fading echoes of "The bastard came up from London with a bloody con bet," not prepared to pay any further penalty.

"The state of this business keeps blowing my mind - we've just been mugged for a bottle," I despondently informed John.

North West Hole-in-One Collections had totalled an impressive £125,000 and we now realised that the freedom to wear rugby shirts and jeans seven days a week and to give bosses the elbow had at long last become reality.

Wednesday 25th September

Phase three of collections meant a South of England sweep that was to take us from Plumpton to Plymouth. The September sun was peeping over the familiar contours of the Sussex Downs as we zapped along, clocking up a further 3000 miles on the Banditmobile mileometer.

... Reputable Chichester Bookie Hugh Gunning hands over a £9,600 kite, offering congratulations.

... Brian Striples' flamboyant image is in tatters, as he pawns jewellery before coughing up £26,000.

... Avon Bookie insists The Duo autograph his copy of The Sun before departing with £8,400.

... A detour through army manoeuvres at Bovington Camp proves to be worthwhile as £1,600 is binned.

... "The Doctor said he needs rest," we are told as wife hands over £7,500.

South of England Hole-in-One collections added another £107,000 - making a grand total of £1/2 MILLION ... and the rest!

BUT ... there was still that £43,000 from the South's Leading Bookmakers.

It was with trepidation that John entered what he assumed was Southampton's Spectrum Racing.

"Bill Slater sold the shop last week, and all ante-post bets are now paid from Spectrum Headquarters," he was promptly told. We anxiously redirected the Banditmobile East towards Brighton.

* The South's leading Racing Service.
* We guarantee you won't get better terms.
* We will guarantee security.
* The only service where you win when you lose.

... we recalled the publicity blurb as we made for Spectrum's colours, keen to embark upon our task.

Requiring a hair cut and shave, Slater was deeply buried into settling bets before our presence rocked him from his chair.

"Where have you been?" the shaken Slater shrieked entering the punting enclosure. "I've advertised in this golf magazine and the Life for you to urgently contact me," he then nervously spluttered. He seemed to be punch drunk as he babbled on ...

* He'd sacked the manager.
* He'd misunderstood the bets anyway.
* A golf limit of £2,000 would now apply.

Printed rules were pinned to the wall and dated July 1989, but some limits had been amended.

The original £100,000 limit per day's business remained unchanged, but previous limits on both football and placepots had been amended to £5,000. In addition a £2,000 golf and snooker limit had been introduced in biro dated 1 March 1991.

"What about your publicity leaflets - they must contravene the Trade Descriptions Act," insisted John producing the Spectrum propaganda.

"Well, it's only an harmless bit of advertising to rake up business," Slater squirmed on. "Where's my winnings?" pleaded John as the whinging bookie made further excuses.

" It's got to the stage where we're talking Mickey Mouse money," he was telling us, sweating up like an unraced two year old. Our frustration was now

"SPECTRUM RACING" BOOKMAKERS
THE SOUTH'S LEADING RACING SERVICE

7 VICTORIA TERRACE HOVE	16 UPPER HAMILTON ROAD BRIGHTON	42 LODGE ROAD SOUTHAMPTON

0273 220918 (all lines)

(We guarantee you won't get better terms or service!)

OFFICES: OPEN AT 9.30a.m. DAILY MONDAY TO SATURDAYS 9.00 SAT	BEFORE 11a.m. EVERYDAY WE ONLY CHARGE "5p" IN THE £1 ON PREPAID TAX BETS AND DURING ALL RACING ONLY 10p IN THE £1 ON PREPAID TAX BETS
GUARANTEED BEST ODDS LAID ON ALL EVENTS. IF IT MOVES WE BET ON IT	1/4 ODDS ON ALL HANDICAPS HORSES OR GREYHOUNDS WITH 6 OR MORE RUNNERS
DEPOSIT AND CREDIT ACCOUNTS OPENED IMMEDIATELY ON "FREE PHONE" BASIS RING AND ASK FOR BILL OR SHARON FOR DETAILS	ALL TELEPHONE BETS IMMEDIATELY TAPED BY VETABET FOR CUSTOMER SECURITY, WITH DAILY SETTLEMENT IF REQUESTED
DAILY " UNBEATABLE" BONUS BETS ALONG WITH UNBEATABLE DAILY SPECIAL OFFERS	1/4 ODDS A PLACE ON ALL T.V. RACES C4/BBC WITH 6 AND MORE RUNNERS
ON SATURDAY MORNINGS ALL BETS STRUCK ON GREYHOUNDS WILL ONLY BE CHARGED AT 5p IN £1 ON PREPAID BETS	"FREE "BOTTLE OF WHISKEY DRAW EVERY WEEK ON ALL LOSING TICKETS
HOT DRINKS ALWAYS AVAILABLE - COMPLIMENTS OF MANAGEMENT	IMMEDIATE PAYOUT OF UP TO £250 SUBJECT TO MANAGERS DISCRETION

"SPECTRUM RACING" BOOKMAKERS -
the only service where you win when you lose!!

* EVERY DAY IS "TAX-FREE" on the following speciality bets. *

MONDAY - PLACEPOT	TUESDAY - UNION JACK'S	WEDNESDAY - LUCKY i5
THURSDAY - ROUND ROBIN	FRIDAY - PATENTS	SATURDAY - SATELLITE SIX

Remember:- "SPECTRUM'S RACING" SERVICE -
leaves others in the stalls, so why not leave a depsoit and give us a ring today

more than apparent, as we realised that apart from hitting Slater with a hammer, our only recourse was again a Green Seal Service arbitration. Unfortunately for us, The Spectrum camp held the Ace

Card, holding both stake money and bundles in winnings.

Some weeks later ... the absence of the Spectrum colours at the Brighton Headquarters was an ominous clue, but that new boat race guaranteed trouble.

"... Of course I can't pay you out - what's it got to do with us?" new owners Royal Racing demanded, as we returned to collect our £43,000 winnings - after The Life had ruled 'We MUST be paid in full.'

Spectrum's Bill Slater had numerous creditors, and had been forced to sell his Southampton Branch in a desperate bid to raise cash; but a kamikaze punting session with the proceeds at a nearby betting shop had completely put the skids under The Spectrum Empire. "He sold us the business for a cup of tea," the Royal spokesman informed us as the issuing of our kite received the official kiss of death. "Can't we even have our stake money back?" came our departing request, as by now we were both feeling quite ill. The bad debts column had suffered a most unpleasant entry. Like any business we anticipated knockers, but £43,000 would surely even have decked Donald Trump.

18. ANYONE CAN MAKE A RICK

The incredible success achieved with the Hole-in-One bet had by now thrown all previous coups into insignificance. Indeed, the years between its conception in '88' and 1990 were in fact the most lucrative of all, but it was not just small independent Bookies during those cavalier days that were sent rocking.

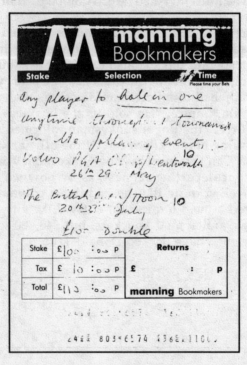

London's biggest independent group, 'Manning Bookmakers' had been approached in '89 regarding a Hole-in-One enquiry and had quoted 10/1. Ten £100 Doubles were laid without flinching, but when boldly returning to the South Chingford Branch the following morning, revised 8/1 odds encouraged further speculation. There was unfortunately a world shortage of Hole-in-Ones that year, but regarding my three winning tickets, Manning's still had to cough up £25,000.

Brent Walker, prior to purchasing the William Hill Organisation, had acquired one hundred and something shops from the group and were also approached in '89. Their generous 25/1 any named Hole-in-One Double quote was promptly reduced to 20/1 amidst an avalanche of interest, but in making the British Open a Banker, we had foolishly placed all our eggs in one basket!

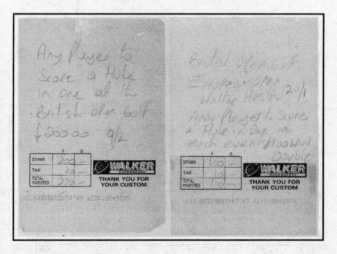

Calamity at Troon meant wads of Walker slips had been reduced to rubble. Never the less, the consolation prize of £5,000 was gratefully accepted.

It was sale time at Corals throughout the '88 season, the pick of the bargains being their 10/1 quote for the Benson & Hedges Tournament taking place at Fulford, near York, and incredible 16/1 British Open odds.

The bookies were slow learners:, 8/1 was still freely available a year later.

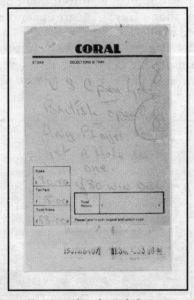

Operations during this fruitful time were handled with the upmost discretion, but eventually word was to spread throughout the Bookmaking business. Inevitably a few hit on the idea of becoming fellow prospectors, but we were concerned that previously classified Hole-in-One information, in inexperienced hands, might cause irreparable damage. However, the biggest threat to Hole-in-One security was press coverage, because any mention of the bet, particularly in the Racing Dailies, would have done Hole-in-One conversion statistics few favours. The Sporting Life Weekender published an article that caused much anxiety at the time, but there was also the danger of a front page explosion.

> ## The Sporting Life Weekender
>
> ● A hole in one can be a costly business for the successful golfer once he reached the 19th. It was also costly for a Yorkshire bookmaker whose assistant laid a visiting punter 14-1 against that happening to anyone in a recent tournament.
>
> You will get that without trouble if you name an individual to do a hole in one, but the
>
> last two televised tournaments have offered proof that an ace is not all too uncommon.
>
> The major bookies reckon it is only a shade over evens, 6-4 at best, for such an eventuality. One even quotes odds-on when the terms are for anyone, unnamed, to get that hole in one. So bookies, who have to pay as laid, should make sure their staff, for whom they are responsible, know the score.

A similar fear determined our policy regarding betting disputes. Apart from writing to the Bookmaker concerned, the issue was rarely pursued.

16 May 1990

Sports (Bookmakers) Ltd
79 Hatfield Road
ST ALBANS
Herts
AL1 4JL

Dear Sirs

A few days prior to this year's Benson and Hedges International Golf
tournament I enquired at your Old Highway, Hoddesdon shop what price you
would be prepared to lay me for any player achieving a hole-in-one,
anytime throughout the tournament. I had in my possession at the time a
couple of betting slips from Bookmakers who had the previous year laid a
bet for a hole-in-one and asked the Manager what price he was prepared to
lay me.

Initially he made a telephone call to his Head Office but apparently the
appropriate person was not available. He then said he was prepared to
lay me £50 tax paid at 12/1 a bet which was then duly struck.

Overjoyed at Andrew Sherbourne's first day triumph, I duly took my ticket
back to your shop to collect my winnings, only to be told that the price
laid was a mistake - the correct odds should have been 5/4 and that you
were only prepared to settle at these odds.

I am sure that as a Bookmaker in your own right you are well aware that
you have no case whatsoever for not paying me my winnings in full. It is
your responsibility to ensure that once quoting a price and laying a bet,
you cannot then change your mind and settle the bet at 5/4 just because
you either feel like it or because another Bookmaker is quoting 5/4.

I now ask for a cheque for £650.00 in full settlement or a full written
explanation as to why you are refusing to settle my bet at the odds laid.

Yours faithfully

J CARTER

SPORTS
(BOOKMAKERS)

79 Hatfield Road, St.Albans, Hertfordshire, AL1 4JL
Telephone: St.Albans (0727) 54421

18th June 1990

Dear Mr Carter

Re: Your Golf bet at our Hoddesdon office.

Thank your for your letter of 16th May 1990 and I must appologise
for not having replied sooner but I have been on Holiday.

I regret that the facts contained in your letter are not accurate
and I would like to put the record straight.

Our office at Hoddesdon is run by a manager who contacted our head
office for a price on this bet.   Our ante post manager was not
available, as we state but our manager was told he can offer you
odds of 12/5   Having struck the bet with you he rang back to
confirm it had been laid, now speaking to the manager reponsible.
The shop manager had mis-heard the instruction of 12/5 and mistakenly
writen 12/1 and was informed that the correct odds were nearer 5/4
but 12/5 was acceptable.

I note you have had similar bets with bookmakers as you have used the
Green Seal Service at Sporting Life to confirm the result.   There was
a warning issued to Bookmakers last year that people were going around
placing similar bets at the wrong odds.   Were you involved with this?

I must draw your attention to rule 7 of our rule book which states
"responsibility cannot be accepted for errors made by either S.I.S or
members of Staff."   and as such can offer you payment at 12/5, which
I am sure you will agree is much better than the correct odds of 5/4.

Should you however wish to go to arbitration on the matter we will be
happy to do so.

Yours sincerely

B N Fulton

Bankers: BARCLAYS BANK PLC

229

19. "IMPROMPTU ORIGAMI LESSONS"

In 1991, despite The Sporting Life's front page ruling that 'Bookies must cough up', many still refused to pay. Subsequently, we entered into many disputes which were adjudicated by The Sporting Life's Green Seal Service. Both parties agreed to abide by their decision and for the most part book-makers were honourable and Paid Up - including arch rival Arthur !

Sadly there was a certain minority who would despite many letters and visits, totally ignore the adjudication in our favour.

However, in 1991 the lid was off the Hole-in-One idea forever, and now with nothing to lose, we decided to relentlessly pursue the culprits like a posse - something this small minority did not bargain for. Unfortunately, Round One of Hole-in-One Objection Action went in the Bookmak-ers' favour due to a performance worthy of the Keystone Cops.

Taking on bookmakers in betting disputes is never an easy undertaking, especially when handling 'Late Entries' to rules and limits. It is a full time task taking on One bookmaker, let alone Twelve! Consequently, many hours were spent laboriously constructing letters worthy of George Carman Q.C.

By the end of October 1991, all Sporting Life

adjudications had been ruled in our favour, and we decided to team up with N.A.P.P. as we thought their affiliation with the Sporting Press exposing the knockers would do our campaign a power of good.

The mountainous piles of files and documentary evidence were wheeled into Lefley N.A.P.P. H.Q. Their own investigations into all cases led to an excellent publicity campaign in the Racing Post.

The winter of '91/'92 was spent ironing out bundles in petrol and hotel bills, touring the coun-

A weekly column by JOHN LEFLEY of the National Association for the Protection of Punters

PUNTERS' PITCH

Lining up those bad bookmakers' licences firmly in our sights

NAPP's executive committee decided earlier this week to help members fight various complaints against off-course bookmakers, including several disputes referred by the punters involved in the 'hole in one' bets earlier this year.

Investigation of these complaints, all of which are well documented, has convinced the committee that these cases must be pursued by every means possible. It is clear that there are some bookmakers who operate licensed betting offices without any proper business experience, any proper knowledge of their trade, or any sense of obligation on bets they have accepted.

Some bookmakers have published limits for bets which they know they have no possibility of ever having the resources to pay out. Others alter their rules retrospectively after a bet, and insist this is reasonable. Others again have no rules displayed at all. Others yet again deny ever laying a bet, despite the written evidence.

It is an appalling catalogue. In the longer term, NAPP will consider how the situation can be improved. What is clear is that magistrates need much more guidance on minimum standards before they issue licences in the first place.

Punters must be protected from the incompetent and barely solvent. NAPP will play its part, but tougher action is needed by magistrates.

It is in the interests of punters, but also of those bookmakers who know their business and their responsibilities, that the situation is radically improved. Few of the bookmakers who have been the subject of the most serious complaints will be members of BOLA or NAB, and NAPP will expect those organisations to support our fight.

NAPP's first action will be to approach all the firms concerned, and remind them yet again of the amounts they owe, to give them a last chance of settling their debts before objections are lodged against renewal of the licences for their shops.

As the law stands, this is the only effective recourse that punters have against the off-course bookmaker, but at least punters have, for the first time, a national organisation to fight their corner.

try's whingers as a last ditch attempt was made to amicably resolve each case: but more often than not "The Green Seal Service" adjudication played the star role in an impromptu origami lesson with the resulting paper aeroplane's maiden flight to the nearest rubbish bin!

The Magistrates' Courts were now our only option, because if a Bookmaker accepts a bet and

consequently refuses to pay, the punter's only recourse is to object to that bookie's Betting Permit, because gambling debts are not legally enforceable.

N.A.P.P. decided to take up the challenge and proceeded to object to all bookmakers involved in the 1992 April Licensing Sessions.

It was agreed that N.A.P.P. would act as our representative, and come April 1992 we headed

North for an objection to be heard by the Ashton-Under-Lyne Magistrates regarding "Steve Davies Racing".

The dispute related to an ante-post sheet displaying 14/1 Hole-in-One odds that had been shown to Mr Davies as a guide to odds that had previously been available. Although about two years out of date (a fact that Mr Davies was made aware of)he had at the time judged the odds to be a reasonable risk and had accepted two £50 bets. With both proving successful, a long battle ensued - with The Sporting Life bombarded with mail regarding the case.

Mr Davies stated he would pay out in full if the Ante Post Sheet was validated, but this was impossible due to its disintegration. His request was in fact irrelevant, because leading Bookmakers had publicly admitted laying similar odds at that time. Mr Davies, in the first instance, approached The Sporting Life and subsequently stated he would abide by the "Green Seal Service" adjudication.

In a ruling dated the 12th November, Mr Davies was told to Pay-Up:
... <u>Our final opinion is that you should settle the bets at 14/1 and like other Bookmakers put the episode down to experience</u>.

... but he still adamantly refused to cough up.

N.A.P.P. Chairman Mark Coton vigorously presented the case during a hearing lasting just over an hour, but as neither party was legally represented, the Magistrates were forced to endure scenes not witnessed since Hancock's Half Hour, with the highlights being Mr Davies approaching the Bench and using the 'Life's' adjudication for his own Defence!

A witness, when asked by Mr Davies whether He would have accepted the wagers, was adamant that, "Anyone who forks out a hundred quid must be a professional punter." When pressed on the issue he replied to Davies' apparent horror "I would never have accepted those bets in a million years."

Sadly, the bench needed only minutes before quashing the objection to the "Steve Davies Racing" licence. The Ashton-Under-Lyne Magistrates appeared both fair and reasonable but were not required to give reasons regarding their decision. To speculate, perhaps 'playing away' from home didn't help or maybe they took the view that two sharp Londoners had travelled North to catch out Northern bookies.

However, only hours prior to the hearing, it had come to light that N.A.P.P. had opposed S.D.R's Shop Licence - which was technically incorrect, as procedure in such circumstances requires an objection to the relevant Betting Permit. Perhaps this may have had some bearing on the outcome.

N.A.P.P. had planned, for the first time in Licensing Renewal history, objections to twelve Bookmakers, but following the day's events, we sadly now faced a dilemma.

NAPP fails to dislodge bookie

By DAVID ASHFORTH

THE National Association for the Protection of Punters yesterday failed in its bid to persuade Ashton-under-Lyne's magistrates not to renew the licence of a bookmaker who had refused to pay out on a hole-in-one golf bet.

The action by NAPP stemmed from last year's well-executed coup by two Essex punters, who travelled the country searching for odds against there being a hole-in-one at major golf tournaments.

Contrary to most people's expectations, a hole-in-one is commonplace. The punters succeeded in obtaining odds much better than the true odds against such an eventuality.

The coup received considerable publicity in The Life and netted a reputed £500,000, but, while most bookmakers paid out, a minority refused to pay, often citing rules relating to the procedures governing the acceptance of bets.

A number of these disputes were referred to The Sporting Life's Green Seal arbitration service. This looked at each case on its merits and, in a majority of cases, found in favour of the punters.

The bookmaker at yesterday's court hearing was Steve Davies Racing, of Droylsden, Tameside.

The dispute concerned bets on the British or United States Open Championships. In each case the stake was £50 and the odds 14-1 against there being a hole-in-one.

Last November, the Green Seal service ruled in favour of the punters. Mr Davies refused to accept the ruling, which is not legally binding.

The objection to Steve Davies' licence was presented by the chairman of NAPP, Mark Coton. He said: "The magistrates have found in favour of the bookmaker, and we must accept that, but it would appear from this ruling that, in future, punters will be at the mercy of incompetent bookmakers."

Coton continued: "It is obviously the last resort to object to a bookmaker's licence, but it is the only sanction left to a punter when a bet has been taken and no payment received."

Davies argued that the punters had misled him over the availability of odds of 14-1.

Yesterday's action was intended to be the first of a series of objections to bookmakers' licences, but Coton said: "We will have to rethink in the light of this ruling. Questions now arise about where punters can go when problems occur and about the need for a code of practice."

● The overwhelming majority of bookmakers and punters accept rulings from the Green Seal Service, which is held in high regard.

There have been notable instances of bookmakers gritting their teeth and paying out thousands of pounds when rulings have gone in favour of the punter.

If a bookmaker's rules name the Green Seal Service as arbiter of disputes, that should be the end of it. However, if a bookmaker rejects a ruling which has gone against him, the punter has no effective recourse.

N.A.P.P. in all cases had opposed Shop Licences so if we were to proceed, the risk of further failure was high. Unfortunately, it was now too late for either John or myself as individuals to use the '92 Renewals Sessions, to lodge objections to Betting Permits relating to the Bookmakers concerned. Alternatively ,we must agree with N.A.P.P. to bow out and live to fight another day.

The latter was the only choice.

PUNTERS' PITCH

THE decision by magistrates in Ashton-under-Lyne to dismiss NAPP's objection to a bookmaker's licence has raised a number of vital issues which must not be allowed to die down.

If a bookmaker takes a bet and refuses to pay out, the punter has no other official sanction but to go to court to object to the permit or licence because gambling debts are not enforceable at law.

This suits nobody. In nearly every case the punter will want his money, not to drive a bookmaker out of business. The law gives him the chance to do the latter, but *not* to get paid.

Quite clearly, a magistrates' court is an utterly inappropriate venue to decide complicated betting matters, as Wednesday's proceedings amply demonstrated. There is hardly a bench in the country that will ever have heard a licence objection, let alone be acquainted with important points of principle in betting.

Sadly, as far as punters are concerned, many bookmakers, big and small, have a principle all of their own and that is 'thou shalt not win' or, to be more precise, 'thou shalt only win as much as we see fit'.

The big bookmakers are guilty more than most of closing accounts, watering down bets and turning punters away. None of this would be tolerated in Australia, where an on-course bookmaker cannot bet unless he guarantees to lay any horse in a race to lose an agreed amount at the given odds to *any* punter who wants a bet. If one man can manage under such conditions, why is it that our major bookmakers cannot?

A product of this 'thou shalt not win' principle is that it is somehow disreputable to have enjoyed a carefully-planned coup, to have pocketed thousands thanks to the generosity, naivety or incompetence of small bookmakers as did the hole-in-one punters whose case NAPP fought.

The magistrates gave no reasons for their decision, which they reached after just three minutes in retirement on Wednesday, despite the hearing lasting the best part of an hour, but it is my guess that they decided that these sharp young men from the South had pulled a fast one and should not be seeking to press hard-working local bookies out of business.

If this is to be the general view, then the law has rendered itself redundant and is an ass. I repeat, the only sanction punters have is to object to a licence. If the law is to decide that this is an inappropriate sanction (as punters would agree it is in most cases; they want their money) then we are all wasting our time.

A second point of principle is vital and straightforward. I quote the National Association of Bookmakers on the hole-in-one issue: 'The day that any bookmaker lays a bet and seeks to change the odds later when he discovers he has made a mistake in his judgment will be a black day indeed for the profession.'

To judge by the papers in NAPP's hands on this issue, this black day has already arrived.

Another point of principle is that the Sporting Life Green Seal service is the accepted final and binding arbiter in disputes between punter and bookmaker.

The fact that a bookmaker can seek a Green Seal ruling, ignore it when it rules against him and hand in the judgment as evidence to *support* his case in a court of law, as happened on Wednesday, is to leave the credibility of the service in tatters.

> *Many bookmakers, big and small, have a principle all of their own and that is 'thou shalt not win'*

A Green Seal ruling has never been legally binding, although the vast majority of punters and bookmakers to have had recourse to it have honoured the judgments even when, as for most of the bookmakers in the hole-in-one cases to have come to NAPP's attention, they have been told to 'put the episode down to experience' and pay up.

Most have paid, some have not—these are the bookmakers we have objected to.

We must now decide whether to proceed with these objections, or to appeal against Wednesday's judgment, or to bow out.

Whatever happens, we must fight for reform. These are the issues.

1: Gambling debts must be recoverable by law. This applies to both punters and bookmakers. If we owe money, we should pay up, other than on grounds for refusal.

2: If a dispute does arise there should be an official body with the power to make binding rulings, including ordering a bookmaker or punter to pay up. Neither the Green Seal service, the secretive Tattersalls Committee nor a court of law are appropriate for this purpose.

3: This new body should be responsible for setting up and enforcing a code of practice for all bookmakers. Failure to adhere to this code would result in objections to permits and licences.

This code should certainly contain minimum payout limits and a requirement to lodge all sales with the new body. Some of the limits enforced by small bookmakers are an insult to the punter and the bookmaking profession. If a bookmaker cannot afford a decent payout he should not be in business.

NAPP also has evidence of bookmakers amending rules after an event to avoid payment, an utterly disgraceful form of behaviour, but easy for the unscrupulous to get away with under the current system.

NAPP would also press strongly for a consumer's charter for punters, including bet guarantees.

The new body would also undertake rigorous checks of bookmakers to weed out the incompetent and fraudulent, especially among credit operations. The unpleasant memory of such companies as TNS and Denver Racing refuses to go away.

4: Unless government pledges support, which is unlikely in the short term, the Levy Board should fund the new body from punters' deductions. Bookmakers should be invited to make ex-gratia contributions to show good faith.

The new body should be accountable to the Levy Board for its expenditure, but it must be utterly independent in its day-to-day decision-making.

5: The Board should be composed of independent figures of utter integrity, including members with experience of betting from all sides of the betting business, punters and bookmakers. It would also need a small executive.

Conclusion: The recent Treasury windfall for racing offers the clear chance to get moving on this matter—provided the will is there.

NAPP plans to write to the Jockey Club, the Levy Board, the Horseracing Advisory Council and The Racehorse Owners' Association. BOLA and the NAB will also be contacted and we call on all punters to express their views in letters to the newspaper, the racing and betting authorities and their MPs.

Hopefully all sides of the industry can unite and get moving on this vital issue.

On 9th April 1992 in the Racing Post Steve Davies had his say:

We acted in good faith says hole-in-one bookmaker

The hole-in-one bookmaker who overcame a licence objection gives his side

FURTHER to all the publicity regarding the coup over the hole-in-one bets and the non-payment of the same by myself and several other bookmakers, I would like to state my reasons.

In my case, it is one of principle that a bet is struck in good faith by both parties, i.e. the bookmaker and the punter.

The basic facts of the case were that he twice came into one of my shops to ask for a price for a hole in one.

On both occasions we declined to take his bet as I know little about golf, but told him should he find a price *nationally* advertised I would match it and lay it. He

then said he had a leaflet from Corals for last year's Open which offered a price for a hole in one.

Albeit that it was supposedly from last year's Open, I took the punter to be acting in good faith, accepting his word that (a) he said he wasn't a gambler but that he and his mate wanted an interest bet on the golf, and (b) that 14-1 had been available last year with Corals.

Before the event took place I discovered I had been misled to have offered the punter this 14-1. If misleading me is not "contravening laying procedures", as stated in the Sporting Life's ruling, then I don't know what is.

Our non-acceptance of the Sporting Life's ruling came after deep consideration but it

was felt the matter had to be aired at a higher level.

The Sporting Life's first opinion was if the price was laid because of a bogus leaflet it wasn't then the bet could be declared void. But their final ruling was we should pay and "put it down to experience".

This remark was quite astonishing. Why should we put it down to experience when we knew we had acted in good faith, yet been deceived.

The punter offered to take odds of 5-1 but we declined. But as our slogan is to offer best price advertised we offered 7-4 which he declined and said he would object to our licence.

We went to court, I did not use a solicitor as I believed I was in the right and would

just state the facts. The case was given a full hearing and lasted nearly 90 minutes. The magistrates retired and returned with their verdict within four minutes rejecting their objections and renewing our licences.

We feel we have now cleared our name in this matter and vindicated ourselves and, far from crying foul and bringing the name of bookmakers into disrepute, it is felt that in our circumstances we were quite right not to settle the bets at 14-1.

Finally, we do agree with Mr Coton of NAPP that some sort of code of legally binding bodies should be set up which protects both interests of punter and bookmakers alike and I'm sure it would be unanimously agreed by all

bookmakers that *all* gambling debts should be recoverable.

FOR AND ON BEHALF OF STEVE DAVIES RACING
Droylsden, Manchester

[JIM CREMIN comments: This bookmaker has a point and, judged by his letter, is a decent man. Nevertheless, he was naive enough to lay the bet and should pay the consequences. Perhaps he won in court because the bench disliked the idea of 'sharp Londoners' catching out 'innocent Northerners'?.

As Mark Coton says, and the bookmaker agrees, the issue now is whether a code of practice is required. Seeing how a small minority of bookmakers do produce ridiculously low limits, or come up with obscure rules AFTER a bet has won, the sooner the better.

In reply 16th April 1992:

The hole-in-one punter has his say

I REFER to the extraordinary letter (Talking Shop last week) from a representative of Steve Davies Racing (SDR) concerning their failure to pay my hole-in-one bet.

It is difficult to understand how SDR can claim to be acting in good faith when, having agreed to abide by a Sporting Life adjudication, they reject the finding when not in their favour. It also defies logic for SDR to claim that they accepted an assurance that a person entering an SP office was not a gambler.

SDR correctly point out

that the justices hearing NAPP's application to have SDR's licence revoked only took minutes to reach a decision after a hearing lasting one and a half hours. This is, surely, a sad indication of the level of care and discretion exercised by the bench.

Jim Cremin's comment that SDR perhaps won because the bench disliked the idea of sharp Londoners catching out innocent Northerners makes a mockery of the concept that everyone is equal before the law.

PAUL SIMONS

237

concerned, explaining that N.A.P.P. were to withdraw objections relating to their Betting Shop Licences ,but went on to say that as individuals we intended to object to all relevant Betting Permits at the earliest opportunity.

Unfortunately,we were snookered until licensing renewal sessions in April the following year. It was frustrating that action could not be taken sooner - and that frustration only intensified as we browsed through numerous files of dispute and disrepute.

We began to write letters to all the Bookmakers

Denholme Racing

BOOKMAKERS

38 MAIN ROAD
DENHOLME
BRADFORD
BD13 4DU

Proprietors: D. and J. M. Loftus

Teh (0274) 834985

29th Sept' 91.

The Sporting Life
Orbit House
1, Fetter Lane
London. EC4A 1AR.

Dear Ms. Cluskey,

re: Mr. P Simons Golf Bet.

I have received from the above named person a threat to object to my betting permit on the grounds that I am not a fit and proper person to hold such a licence.

This is due in part to my not receiving a reply to my letter of the 24th of July 1991. In it I explained how an apparently decent looking chap came into my office asking for a price on a 'hole in one' which obviously I was unable to offer as I had never laid such a bet before. That was Mr Simons first hurdle overcome, as he pointed out in the Sun newspaper, one man operations were targeted as they had carried out the same'con' the previous year, on the 'Big Four' and had been seen for what they are. Rather then turn him down flat I said I would ring Corals for a quote if he was prepared to accept the odds they were offering. He agreed and I made the call. They simply said they were not laying odds on that particular bet. I then suggested that I ring Hills and once again he agreed, all the time knowing that I would not raise a price. After ringing Ladbrokes and a local bookmaker I decided that as he seemed a 'straight' sort of person I would ask if he had made the bet before. He told me that he had a similar bet last year and was offered between 6/1 & 16/1. He ommited to mention that he had placed similar bets in my area that very same day at various prices.

I said that as he had been given the prices he quoted then I would give him 7/1. Obviously Mr Simons was happy to accept any odds above 10/11 which were the realistic odds. My appeal to you rests on the fact that Mr Simons deliberately, if not fraudulently, with his act, obtained from not only Denholme Racing but many of my friends, odds of a truly unrealistic size and by his own admission achieved his goal of extorting money with his shadey ploy. Should the 'Green Seal Service' rule in favour of these two underhanded objects then I will assume you do not wish to see fair play between bookmaker and punter. In the scheme of things the £400.00 is a small amount but it is a big principle. They must not prevail!

Yours Faithfully,

(Proprietor & Licensee)

238

Denholme Racing

38 MAIN ROAD
DENHOLME
BRADFORD
BD13 4DD

Proprietors D. and J. M. Loftus

BOOKMAKERS

Tel: (0274) 834985

18th October 91

Dear Mr. Simons,

I thank you for your letter of the 15th of October and indeed you are
right in the judgement given by the Sporting Life favoured yourself and
your accomplice. However, you will note that no cheque is present in this
envelope and the reason for this is that Denholme Racing went out of business last Saturday, the 12th October 1991. This can be verified by H.M.
Customs & Excise, Westfield House, Bradford.

I can only say how extremely sorry I am that it is financially impossible
to pay you at this time as my unemployment benefit consists of only a
National Insurance stamp and so consequently I have no income whatsoever
nor do I have any assetts which I could realise in order that I can pay
you your £400, which to my mind you fraudulently obtained. Obviously, I
must be wrong and I am delighted that you won your decision with the 'Green
Seal Service' but it does sadden me to know that I cannot uphold my obligation to the pair of you. Suffice it to say that if I should find any form
of work I will do my utmost to ensure that you are paid as it is a matter
of honour and I cannot stand people who do not act in an honourable way,
especially those who are deceitful.

Yours Sincerely,

David Loftus.

Although much of our pain was self inflicted, we
rallied and planned a new strategy - but first, a call
at the Sun's Wapping HQ was a must ....

WE NAME BOOKIES WHO WON'T PAY IN £85,000 COUP

SPOILSPORT bookies are refusing to hand over £85,000 to the Hole-in-One gang who pulled off one of the biggest stings in gambling history.

And today we name the guilty 11 of 135 firms hit by the £500,000 coup who held back winnings.

They did it even though an independent arbitration service has said they should pay up.

Former betting office managers Paul Simons, 36, and John Carter, 30, from Essex, teamed up four years ago to plan the sting.

They cashed in on the ignorance of small-time bookies who didn't know that holes-in-one happen at nearly every golf tournament.

Suckers

They drove 212,000 miles and visited more than 1,000 bookies to find their 135 suckers.

The pair got odds of up to 100-1 from the small-timers while the big bookmaking chains were only offering even money.

They wagered £30,000

WINNERS . . . John (left) with Paul

By JOHN KAY

in a series of single and double bets. When aces occurred at five tournaments they expected a £500,000 pay-out—from a perfectly legal coup.

But John said: "The bookies resorted to every kind of trick to try to wriggle out of paying."

The duo appealed to The Sporting Life—the bible of the betting industry—for help.

The paper's independent Green Seal arbitration service ruled in their favour in every

case. But they are still owed £84,620 by 11 bookies who refuse to pay up.

Paul said: "The owner of one chain which owed us £43,000 has sold up without paying."

One of the gang's biggest hits was on Arthur Whittaker's betting shop in Derby.

They got odds of 100-1 against a hole-in-one at the British Open in July last year. They staked £50 and paid tax of £5. Brian Marchbank obliged with a hole-in-one at the 12th on the first day—

netting the gang £5,000.

They also won another £10,000 from Mr Whittaker on holes-in-one at 'other tournaments—but were only paid after the Green Seal ruling.

Licences

The gang are now opposing renewal of the licences of the 11 bookies who won't pay.

They have also called in the National Association for the Protection of Punters.

NAPP chief Mark Coton says of the sting: "Many of these bookies

were naive and incompetent. But in Britain there is no law for the enforcement of gambling debts."

Paul and John were flooded with offers after The Sun exclusively revealed how they pulled off the coup.

Now their classic sting is being turned into a 90-minute film.

And they are planning another big sting for next year.

Paul said: "We are confident that we can break our record and make more than £500,000 from it."

NO WIN BOOKIES LTD	
SPECTRUM RACING Southampton	£43,000
STACEY RACING Warrington	£1,010
A & S RACING Warrington	£810
ALEX ANDERSON Leftwich	£1,040
C RACING, now owned by GS RACING SERVICES, Wigan	£6,250
FRAYNE BOOKMAKERS Golborne, Gtr Manchester	£1,200
TONY AMBROSE Adlington, Lancs	£820
MIKE LANGLEY (BOOKMAKERS) Wolverhampton	£14,000
KISMET RACING Portsmouth	£14,990
JIM LYN Aston in Makerfield	£600
SDR RACING Droylsden, Manchester	£1,800

BAD LOSERS . . . the bookies who welshed

THE SUN SAYS

Bookies are lousy losers

The Sporting Life

WHAT'S the fastest mover at any race course? A bookie as he slips your fiver into his satchel.

But when it comes to paying out, some of them refuse at the first.

Two bright punters put together a well researched plan to bet on holes-in-one at major golf tournaments. They lay their savings of £30,000 in a brilliant series of bets across the country and they are set to pick up £500,000.

But actually wrenching their legitimate winnings from the grasp of mean, twisting, bookies is proving impossible.

ELEVEN bookmakers are disgracing the turf by refusing to hand over a total of £85,000 owed to the lads.

.... and within two months, a 10 Point Charter had been drawn up demanding stringent controls to protect the punter.

A BET-TER DEAL

A CHARTER has been drawn up to force bookies into giving punters a fairer deal.

The move comes after the scandal of spoilsport bookies who refused to hand over £85,000 winnings to the Hole-In-One Gang.

The ten-point charter is designed to stop bookies trying to wriggle out of paying when punters beat them fair and square. The newly-formed National Association for the Protection Of Punters stepped in after The Sun exclusively revealed the plight of the Hole-In-One duo.

By JOHN KAY

Former betting office managers Paul Simons, 34, and John Carter, 30, from Essex, teamed up four years ago to plan the golf sting.

Coup

Last year they won over £500,000 with a series of bets on holes in one at big golf tournaments.

They cashed in on the ignorance of small-time bookies who didn't know holes-in-one happen at nearly every tournament.

But when the duo set out to collect their winnings from the perfectly legal coup they hit a wall of resistance.

Eleven of the 135 firms stung by the duo are still refusing to pay them a total of £85,000 in winnings.

The charter says bookies must honour all bets once they've been accepted—and they can't plead ignorance to try and avoid dodging payouts.

Now NAPP wants its Charter displayed and adopted in all Britain's 10,000 betting shops.

NAPP chairman Mark Coton said: "It is high time something was done to protect punters from ignorant and unscrupulous bookmakers.

"The recent experience of the Hole-In-One punters has exposed grave flaws in the system.

Arrogant

"Gambling debts are not recoverable by law and punters are left out in the cold.

"A bookmaker failing to pay out after accepting a bet is a grave matter.

"But the law and the Jockey Club stand idly by."

Mr Coton added: "Punters must be protected from fraudulent and incompetent bookmakers.

"The seedy back street welcher is alive and well and must be hunted down.

"But the big bookmakers are not immune from criticism.

"They have an iron grip on the industry but there are no checks on their often arrogant use of their power."

NAPP was formed in September and has a 12-man committee which is supported by donations from members.

University law graduate Mr Coton said: "We want the charter to be honoured by all bookmakers.

"Failure to do so should mean immediate termination of a bookmaker's right to bet.

"The time has come for a fair deal for Britain's millions of ordinary punters."

Wriggle

Last night the Hole-In-One duo Paul and John welcomed the charter and said: "Collecting our winnings has been like getting blood from a stone.

"The bookies are only too glad to take your bets.

"But when it comes to paying out, all that most of them can do is squeal and wriggle."

HONEST JOHN BOOKIE

1 Once a bet is accepted, it must be honoured.

2 No bookmaker can plead ignorance to try to dodge paying out.

3 Bookmakers' rules must be scrutinised to expose get-out clauses.

4 Bookies must be banned from changing rules to avoid payment.

5 A minimum £2,000 pay-out when bookies say they can't pay the full amount.

6 A bookmaker's financial status examined before a licence is granted.

7 Punters not to be banned from betting shops without proper reasons.

8 Bookies guarantee to take bets on any event on which they offer odds.

9 New official body to rule on betting disputes.

10 The Horse Levy Body to use part of the betting tax to protect punters.

Did they welch on you?

THE Sun wants to hear from punters who have been diddled or welshed on by bookies.

We'll investigate complaints and build a dossier to assist NAPP in their campaign for a fair deal for punters. Send your stories to: BOOKIE, The Sun, 1 Virginia St, London, E1 9BD.

In July 1992 another defaulter was added to the list - East Preston Racing.

16th September 1991

The Sporting Life
(Green Seal Service)
1 New Fetter Lane
London EC4 1AR

Dear Sir

In mid-April this year I went to the licensed betting premises of East Preston Racing Services, 131 North Lane, East Preston, Rustington, Sussex and asked the owner what price he would be prepared to offer me for any player to score a Hole in One in the forthcoming Benson & Hedges Golf tournament at St Mellon, Cornwall.

He said he would lay me 25/1 on any named tournament during the year, and I duly placed four tax paid bets as per copies enclosed. When I returned to the shop I handed the owner the first ticket regarding the Benson & Hedges at St Mellon. I was then promptly told by the owner that he had misquoted the odds and also misread the bets, and was going to settle my bets as follows: that the odds laid were for an individual player to score a Hole in One which he said was 25/1, and so the bets were to be settled in proportion to how many players took part in each event. There were 150 players in the Benson & Hedges tournament so he has settled the bet as £1.33 on each player. So on the copy enclosed he has personally written a return of £34.84 (he could not find my top copy at the time) and has duly kept the rest of my stake money. How can any person lay out a stake of £220.00 only to get a return of £34.84?

Would you please give me a ruling on the circumstances given.

Yours faithfully

J CARTER

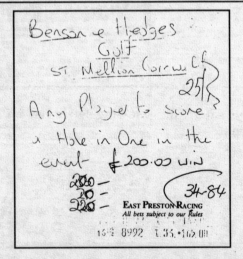

242

Sporting Life, not surprisingly, said Cough Up! A copy of their opinion was sent to East Preston Racing with this covering letter.

```
The Proprietor
East Preston Racing Services
131 North Lane
East Preston
RUSTINGTON
Sussex.


15th October 1991                              My Ref: JCeprL01



Dear Sir,

                          UNPAID BETS

I refer to your failure to pay me the sum of £18,200.00 in respect of
hole-in-one golf bets placed with you on 16th April 1991.

I enclose herewith a copy of a letter dated 16th September which I
wrote to the Sporting Life, Green Seal Service, and a copy of their
reply dated 23rd September. You will see from this that they do not
accept your absurd interpretation of the bets, stating that each bet
should be paid to the full stake at the odds laid.

In the circumstances, I should be grateful to receive the sum of
£18,200.00 from you within ten days of the date hereof. Should the
monies due not be paid within the time stated, I will take the
earliest opportunity to object to your bookmaker's permit in
proceedings before your local magistrates.

Yours faithfully,



J CARTER.
```

Days later, the following letter fell on John's doormat.

Dear Sir,

With regards to your letter dated 21.10.91. I would take
this opportunity to point out, that we had a disagreement
on the first bet, you placed with me. When you left my shop
on your last visit, I was given to understand, that you
would be returning on the following Monday with a draught
of a letter, to the 'Sporting Life'. It was also understood that
the remaining wages were void.

I understand your reason for not wanting to gain adjudication, before your other wages , elsewhere had been collected. In the circumstances I feel unable to change my
reading of the situation regarding myself.

As a means of settling this matter amicably I sugest, that
we settle, as following, without predudice. I will endeav-
our to pay the first wager in full and void the other three
wages.

It will take me a few weeks to dispose of some assets, to
pay this out. Meanwhile I have returned your stakes in full
on all four wages, and await your reply.

and John's reply ....

18th November, 1991

East Preston Racing
131A North Lane
East Preston
West Sussex

Dear Sir,

The betting dispute that currently exists between us has recently been
placed in the hands of N.A.P.P. whom I understand will be contacting you
shortly.

Following the receipt of your letter dated the 4th November, we have been
advised by both our legal adviser and N.A.P.P. to return your cheque to you
as your offer is not acceptable.

When I was at your premises attempting to collect my winnings you stated
that you were not interested in the Sporting Life's opinion and would only
settle the bets in proportion or alternatively you would be prepared to
void all the bets. Indeed this would still appear to be the case by the
receipt of your cheque for £770.00, the original stake money.

Furthermore, after about one hour of causing me much embarrassment in front
of your other customers, I left your premises in a demeaned condition with
the matter clearly still unresolved.

Yours faithfully,

J CARTER

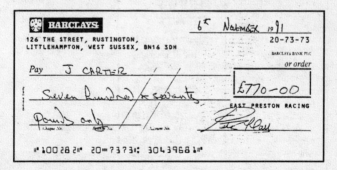

In April 1992, John received an emotional appeal
from the proprietor's wife, explaining that her husband had severe financial problems and was suf-

245

fering poor health. It also transpired that he was to re-finance the business, and the intended objections, if pursued, would inevitably put fund raising efforts under threat. Later that month, a settlement was agreed and a post dated cheque issued.

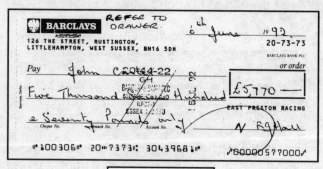

Bookie's hole-in-1 runner

By JOHN KAY

THE hole-in-one gang, who scooped over £500,000 in golf bets, have been diddled out of another £18,000 by a welshing bookie.

When the pair, who bet on holes in one at golf, went for their £18,200 winnings they were offered £34.84p.

Ex-betting shop managers Paul Simons, 36, and John Carter, 30, from Essex, staked £770 with East Preston Racing, West Sussex.

They bet on a series of holes-in-one at golf tournaments. They cashed in on small-time bookies' ignorance of the game and got odds up to 100-1.

The paltry offer from East Preston Racing has taken winnings held back by bookies to £100,000. Now the firm has gone bust

246

April 1993...

The groundwork for the Permit Objections had been completed by London solicitors, and a Manchester based barrister was engaged to represent us for a limited but concise campaign.

Some people may wonder why we should pursue bookmakers, when in some instances little cash was involved? There were many points of principle at stake, the main one being ..... Why should reputable bookies Pay-Up, and the whingers be allowed to escape ?

The first objection concerned 'C' Racing (now owned by GS Racing Services), but upon taking advice, this was settled out of court.

A statement agreed by us and the Bookmakers, at Wallasey Magistrates Court, 8th April 1993 ....

"A bona-fide dispute between the parties has been resolved to their mutual satisfaction and all objections have been withdrawn. "

However, on Thursday 13th April 1993, Wigan Magistrates Court was the venue for objections against the Betting Permits held by Tony Ambrose and Norma Francis Frayne. (Frayne Bookmakers)
With Steve Davies spectating, the first case to be heard by the bench concerned Bolton's Ambrose - a case with little chance of an out-of-court settlement.

Ambrose had been another bookie who had not shied from speaking to the press.

The Sporting Life - 27th July 1991.

Layers at odds over hole-in-one payout

Tony Ambrose, who runs a shop in north Bolton, Lancashire, is one who has no intention of settling the bet.

He said yesterday: "This man has done a marvellous job. He had two bets with us of £50 at 25-1, but he hustled us for the price by showing us some old newspaper cuttings about Corals laying him 33-1 a few years ago. It was a mistake on our part to give him the 25-1 and I don't intend to pay out— I can't afford to.

"One of my rules states that ante-post prices are laid subject to them being correct at the time and, for me, the cashier made an error on the bet. If The Life's Green Seal Service says I have to pay out, then I will delete that service from my rules and abide by my own.

"The day before the Volvo, Trevino bookmakers were offering just 7-4 for a hole-in-one and 5-2 on for no hole-in-one. I will pay out on Trevino's price of 7-4 and if the man isn't satisfied, we could negotiate on the price."

Contrary to his comments, Tony had in fact laid two £10 bets at 25/1 (not two bets of £50 as stated) and he had most certainly not been shown some old newspapers "about Coral's laying .... 33/1 a few years ago." Furthermore, it had been Mr Ambrose himself who quoted the odds and then accepted both bets, not one of the cashiers. He concluded by stating that he had no intention of abiding by any 'Green Seal Service adjudication' but a letter was never the less sent, seeking their views on the facts stated. Mr Ambrose's own National Association of Bookmakers expressed their opinion on the matter on the 1st August .....

"The Bolton Bookmaker who was quoted in The Life as saying that having laid two £50 bets at 25/1, he was prepared to settle them at 7/4 ,has done little for the trust and confidence upon which Betting and Bookmak-

ing is built. To make it worse, he went on to say that if The Life's Green Seal Service says he should pay out - which it did - then he will delete that service from his rules and abide by his own."

In a letter published in The Sporting Life a week later Ambrose made his reply ....

Sporting Life 8th August.

Rules are the bookies' lifeline

AFTER 15 years running small-turnover betting offices, I now find myself at loggerheads with the National Association of Bookmakers and their latest Boarderline article.

The rules every bookmaker displays in his office are his lifeline. My Rule Three states: "Ante-post prices and board prices laid subject to them being current at the time. Should mistakes be made by either party then the next available correct show will be paid."

This useful rule enables a small bookmaker like myself to operate 99.9 per cent of the time

without disputes. Moreover, it is usually applied when fraudsters come into the area to pick off the unsuspecting bookmaker in a tried-and-tested routine.

Does the NAB representative believe the Big Three's prices are never amended?.

Misrepresentation and deception will be fought against by big and small bookmakers alike, with or without the help of the NAB or The Sporting Life Green Seal Service.

TONY AMBROSE

Chorley, Lancashire.

In response to my letter to the 'Green Seal Service' they reiterated their front page ruling, stating "there is a world of difference between a palpable error and an error of judgement" and adding "Mr Ambrose has been roundly criticised by his peers, who seem very concerned about the effect his action may have on the reputation of Bookmakers in general."

On the 18th April 1992, The Sun Newspaper named Tony Ambrose as one of the non -payers. The expose was picked up by the Racing Pundit John McCririck, who launched a blistering attack on the bookies that very morning on his Channel 4 morning line slot. This apparently prompted Mr Ambrose to pen a letter to myself and to send a copy to John McCririck...

Tony Ambrose,
Turf Accountants,
3 Station Road,
Adlington,
Lancs PR7 4LA.
19th April, 1992.

Copy to John McCririck,
C4 Racing.

Dear Mr. Simons,

Re: Hole-in-one Golf Bets

Please find enclosed a cheque for £55 in settlement of your golf bets in accordance with my rules. Rule ③ of which states:-

Antepost prices and board prices are laid subject to them being correct at the time. Should mistakes be made by either party then the next available correct show will be paid (2 x £10 x 7/4 bets in your case)

I also believe that the Sporting Life Green Seal service ruling has also been complied with.

If I have been seen to be guilty of "naivety and incompetence" then so be it. As a matter of principal, the balance of the £520 you say I owe you will be passed onto charity.

In this way, I will have paid up and in doing so will, using a statement published in the Sporting Life "put it down to experience".

Tony Ambrose.

250

On 13th April 1993.

Wigan Magistrates refused to renew Anthony Ambrose's Bookmaker's Permit, and awarded £350.00 costs.

The Licence was also not renewed.

Frayne Bookmakers settled out of court.

WELSHING BOOKIE FORCED TO PAY UP

By JOHN KAY

Hole in One Gang's revenge

THE hole-in-one gang who won £500,000 in golf betting coups have forced a welshing bookie to cough up.

They squeezed £3,000 from a firm that refused to pay out by threatening to oppose its gambling licence.

John Carter and Paul Simons made their fortune betting on golfers scoring holes-in-one in tournaments.

Small bookies gave odds of up to 100-1 — not realising the real chances were as low as evens.

GS Racing, of Billinge, Merseyside, were among about ten firms who refused to stump up a total of £80,000 when the truth dawned on them.

John, 34, and Paul, 38, opposed the bookie's betting licence when it came up for renewal at Wallasey magistrates court.

They hired barrister David Pickup in their bid to recover £6,250 they say they were owed from a series of double bets on golf aces. Minutes before the case was due to start, GS Racing agreed an out-of-court settlement of £3,000.

A statement agreed by the duo and the bookies said: "A bona-fide dispute between the parties has been resolved to their mutual satisfaction and all objections have been withdrawn."

John and Paul, former betting office managers from Essex, will today oppose the licences of two more northern bookies who refused to pay.

John said last night: "There is still money outstanding. We are determined to get it."

<u>NO WIN BOOKIES LTD - UPDATE AUGUST 1993.</u>

<u>OWED.</u>

SPECTRUM RACING - Brighton
Owner fled business,
 sold up without paying............................... £43,000

STACEY RACING - Warrington
100/1 offered, two £5 bets placed.
Only prepared to settle at 7/4 ....£1,010

HORSE FAIR - St Helena, North Yorks
£50 at 14/1 laid,
only prepared to settle at 7/4 ....£750

A & C RACING - Warrington
50/1 offered, one £10 bet placed,
Only prepared to settle at 7/4 ....£510

MIKE LANGLEY BKRS - Willenhall Road,
Wolverhampton
Winning bets amounted to £14,000
Subsequently agreed settlement at £5,600
due to shop payout limits and
financial difficulties -
Eventually sold up without paying...........£14,000

JIM LYN - Aston-in-Makerfield
5/1 offered, two £50 bets placed,
refused to pay, subsequently did not renew
Betting Permit or Shop Licence,
- April 1992 - £600

ALEX ANDERSON - Leftwich, Cheshire
Offered 25/1, two £20 bets placed .
Initially voided wagers, subsequently
offered £250 in settlement £1040

STEVE DAVIES RACING - Droysden, Manchester
Proceedings regarding an objection to the
Betting Permit applicable to Steve Davies
April 1993 were suspended when they failed
to reapply £1,500

KISMET RACING - Portslade
Bankrupt, did not pay £15,000

BEIGHTON RACING - Beighton Sheffield
applicable Betting Permit CH PAYNE
£100 at 14/1 laid, only prepared to settle
at 6/4 ....£1,500

J.D. & R. HOGG BKRS - Seahouses,
Northumberland
14/1 offered, one £50 bet placed,
Only prepared to settle at 11/8 ....£750

STOCKPORT RACING - Stockport
Two £50 bets at 10/1 accepted,
paid out on first wager but refused
to honour the second bet
- Settled out of court 26th April 1993 ....

A FINANCIAL HEALTH WARNING.

Betting can be great fun - but you can easily get into real trouble if you don't make sure you stay in control.

Here are our 10 Golden Rules for getting the most out of a flutter.

1) Never gamble with money you can't afford to lose - and NEVER EVER borrow money to have a bet.

2) Keep a record of every bet, noting how much was won or lost.

3) You are guaranteed to lose if you bet on every event. Select carefully instead.

4) Never chase your losses - when you are on a losing streak, moderate your bets until your luck changes.

5) Treat your betting as a 12-month operation. Record what you have in January 1 and what you have in takings or losses by December 31.

6) A good horse racing bet is the Tote Placepot - picking horses which will be in the frame in the first six races at a meeting. The Placepot can occasionally pay freak high returns.

7) The next best horse racing bet is the Tote Jackpot - picking the winners of the first six races. After big meetings like Ascot or Cheltenham, the jackpot can be huge.

8) Never place an accumulator with a small bookie. They probably have low payout limits hidden in the small print of their rules, and - as we have seen - some back street bookies reprint their rules to dodge paying out.

9) Concentrate on sports where you have some knowledge and experience. This way you have a better chance of beating the bookie's odds compiler.

10) If you ask for a £500 bet on a really good thing and the bookie says he will only let you have £100 - bite his hand off and take it. You can always place the rest with other bookies, can't you?

We hope that you have enjoyed
the ride on the Hole- in-One
ROLLERCOASTER.

But ... what's this ... ?

Who needs these 1000/1 chances ...?

GOLF BET PAIR IN ARREST BUNGLE

EXCLUSIVE By JOHN KAY

THE hole-in-one golf duo who stung bookies for £500,000 were arrested on suspicion of carrying out a £10,000 armed robbery, it was revealed last night.

Paul Simons, 36, and John Carter, 30, were locked in police cells for seven hours before being released without charge.

The duo had been forced to stop their Ford Sierra on the M23 in Sussex. They were quizzed over a hold-up in Reigate, Surrey, earlier in the day, in which a Sierra Cosworth was used.

Now the ex-betting office managers plan to sue for wrongful arrest.

Paul, of Essex, said: "We make our money by stinging bookies, not armed robbery."

The pair won a fortune placing bets on aces at golf tournaments.

Keep prospecting!

GLOSSARY

ACE: Hole-in-One
BIRDIE: Score of one stroke under par for a hole.
BOGEY: Score of one stroke over par.
EAGLE: Score of two strokes under par.
MATCH PLAY: A contest which is determined by holes won or lost.
PAR: Expected standard score.
TEE: Area of golf course from which the first stroke of a hole is made.
THREE BALL: Three players playing a round of golf together
TIE: Score the same as another competitor.

MONEY TERMINOLOGY

£1 = Stripe/Nicker
£2 = Bottle
£3 = Carpet
£4 = Ruof
£5 = Jacks
£6 = Tom Mix
£7 = Neves
£8 = TH
£9 = Clothes line
£10 = Tenner/cockle
£20 = Score
£25 = Pony
£50 = Bullseye/Nifty
£100 = One'r/Long 'Un

£500 = Monkey
£1000 = Grand
RAND: Monetary unit of South Africa

HOLE-IN-ONE PHRASEOLOGY

ARBITRATION: Hearing and settling of a dispute by an impartial referee chosen by both sides.
BANDIT POWER: An unexplained force that energises when placing bets.
BAR OF SOAP: A very small amount of money.
BIN: Cash collected, or secured.
BLOWN OUT: Excessive stakes resulting in bet being refused.
BOATRACE/
BOATOMETER: Person's face or facial expression.
BONA-FIDE : Honest or genuine.
CHUNK : A large amount of money.
CLOCKED: Noticeed, observeed, seen or spot.
CLUSTER-BOMB: Doubles and multiple bets.
CODGER: Elderly man.
DE MOB OVERCOAT: Complimentary garment supplied to serviceman on release from the Armed Forces.
DWELL-UP-STAKES: Intentionally waste time.
FALL OUT ZONE: Region of Great Britain not recommended for Hole-in-One punters.
FUNK: Hope, pray etc.
KAMIKAZE: Undertaken in the knowledge that a course of action will result in calamity.
KEYS JOB: Presentation of betting shop keys in lieu of debt.
KITE: Cheque.
LEAVING IT BEHIND: Losing money.
LUMPY: A large stake bet.

NAUSE: Nuisance.

NOM DE PLUME: Alias or fictional name.

OCHE: Darts mark on the floor behind which a player must stand.

ORIGAMI: Japanese art of paper folding.

PIPE: Look, notice, observe, see or spot.

READIES: Cash, money.

RICK: Mistake, error.

SCHLAP: Long drive or walk.

SPIEL: Plausible talk.

SPLODGER: Large staking gambler.

STITCH-UP: Taking advantage of another person's naivety.

STUMER: Bad or useless.

SWEAT-UP: Discomfort and stress felt when awaiting the outcome of a bet.

SWEETENER: A bet placed as a diversionary tactic.

TELETHON: Numerous and/or long telephone calls.

TWO-UP: Popular Australian game, where fortunes are gambled upon the spin of a coin.

WAD: Bundle of cash.

YE OLDE: Days of yore.

BETTING TERMINOLOGY

ACCUMULATOR: A bet of four or more selections in which the total returns are invested on each successive selection. Other common names are Accer, 4 Fold, 5 Fold, 5 timer etc.

ANTE POST: Betting on an event well in advance of it taking place.

BANKER: A highly fancied selection which is often the cornerstone of a multiple bet..

BEESWAX/AJAX: Betting Tax.

BET A THIRTY THREE PONYS: £25 bet at 33/1 odds.

BOTTLE: 2/1 or £200.

BOTTLE-ON : Odds of 1/2.

CARPET: 3/1 or £300

CHECKED-UP: A greyhound racing term. To thwart or hinder.

CORRECT SCORE ODDS: Predict the exact score in an event.

DOUBLE: A bet involving two selections in which the total return from the first selection is invested onto the second selection.

EACH OF TWO: Two possible outcomes with an equal probability of success.

EIGHTEEN THOUSAND TO TWO: £2000 bet at 9/1 odds.

ELEVEN HUNDRED TO TEN: £1000 at 11/10 odds.

FACES: Known shrewd or 'live' punters.

FLIMPING: Giving under the odds or under paying.

FOURTEEN FIFTIES: £50 bet at 14/1 odds.

FRAME: First few past the post in an event.

GET-ON: Eager to place bet.

GET-OUT: Bet struck to recover previous loses.

GONE THROUGH THE CARD: Backed every winner in every race.

GREEN SEAL: Arbitration service offered by The Sporting Life regarding betting disputes.

HAVE IT OFF/CRACK IT: A big win.

HEDGING: Bookmakers lessening the potential liabilities by themselves backing the selection.

"IN RUNNING": Betting on the outcome of an event during the progression of play.

IRONED OUT: Lose money.

IRONED OUT A CHUNK: Huge financial loss.

JACKPOT: Tote Bet, pick the winners of the first six races at the jackpot meeting. If the jackpot is not won, the pool is carried forward to the next nominated fixture.

JOLLY'S: Favourite.

KNOCK/KNOCKERS: Owe money, defaulters.

LAY: To accept a bet at offered odds.

LAYING OFF: Bookmakers lessening the potential liabilities by giving all or part of the bet they've laid to another firm.

LIFE: The Sporting Life daily newspaper.

"NO OFFERS": Near certainty.

ODDS: Ratio showing the probability of something happening.

ODDS ON: Odds of less than Even Money.

'PICK 6': A popular Tote accumulator bet available on U.S.A. racecourses.

PLACEPOTS: Tote Bet, select horses to be placed in the first six races (or to win in races of two to four runners). The placepot operates at all meetings.

POST: The Racing Post daily newspaper.

PRESS-UP: Increase stake of a fancied bet.

SINGLE: A bet of one selection.

S.I.S.: Satallite Information Service.

SPREAD BETTING: Profits or loses are decided by betting either higher or lower to a given figure.

SUPER YANKEE: Multiple bet consists of 26 bets involving five selections in different events, i.e. ten doubles, ten trebles, five four folds plus one five fold.

TANK: Reserves of cash.

THE WICK: Hackney Greyhound Stadium.

TO MAKE THE FRAME/IN THE FRAME: First few past the post in an event.

TREBLE: A bet involving three selections in which the total returns are invested onto each successive selection.

TRI-CAST: A computer calculated bet, requiring the selection of the first three in correct order in handicaps of eight or more declared runners.

"TWO ON": Odds of 1/2.

VALUE: Securing generous odds.

VEGAS MEGABUCKS POOL: One armed bandits operated by participating Nevada Casinos which are linked by a computer.

YANKEE: Multiple bet consists of eleven bets involving four selections in different events, i.e. six doubles, four trebles, one four fold.

3/1: each of 6 betting show; 6 runners all offered at 3/1 odds.

No more excuses

LIKE many others I have been following the saga of the hole-in-one coup with great interest.

Given that you yourselves have stated that there is no reason for a bookmaker to withhold payment, that many bookmakers have promptly paid up and any punter would expect to be paid up in the same circumstances, why not preempt the intransigents by passing judgment on the front page and continuing to publicise the individuals concerned.

I am not au fait with the legal niceties, but I cannot see how anyone can keep a licence when they will only pay out if it suits them.

As all was correct and above board, there is no argument and, if anything, interest must be due to the "winners".

PETER REID

London, E15.

WELL DONE my Sun for exposing the 11 whingeing bookies who refused to pay out for the hole-in-one coup (*The Sun, April 21*).

Most punters such as me lose to people like them all the time, but when anyone finds a way to beat them they scream or refuse to pay.

Mrs C. FRENCH, Barkingside, Essex

Hole-in-one payouts due

I READ with some amusement about the continuing saga of the so-called "hole-in-one scam".

I was a "victim" of this bet a few years ago and laid £50 at 20/1. I accepted the bet in good faith and paid the same.

What concerns me is the screams of the bookmakers who state they will not pay at the odds they have laid. Surely, if they lay the odds and take the bet, they must pay. It doesn't really matter what Hills' or Ladbrokes' or Trevino's odds are.

There is only one animal worse than a welching punter and that's a welching bookie!

JIM GRAY

Dunblang.

Effrontery of layers

THE effrontery of bookmakers never ceases to enrage me, wanting as usual to change the rules if they are in danger of losing.

Are we to believe that if the bets had gone down, Arthur Whittaker, who had quoted large odds about a hole in one, would have diligently hunted down the poor punters to return their stakes as the bets had been accepted in error?

IAN ATKINSON

Wirral, Merseyside.

Pay up, bookies

ONCE again we see the bookies crying "foul" just because they made an error.

I refer to the hole-in-one saga reported in The Sporting Life this week.

When a "stranger" places a bet at fixed odds and it wins, and the bookmaker then realises the price was embarrassingly generous, they declare it was an "organised coup". What nonsense!

If Mr Whitaker has not trained his representative correctly, then it is his responsibility.

If the bet had not won, would the punter be allowed to say "Sorry, I made a mistake, I only meant to bet £5 and not £50, so can I have £45 back?"

So, fair's fair, the bet was taken at those odds and should be honoured. The bookmakers should pay up and stop whingeing.

DENNIS SUTTON

Ruislip, Middlesex.

We thank you all for your generous support.

IN AMERICA

by

"DANIEL"

Why are the F.B.I. and the Mafia both in a race to find Daniel?

Why does the beautiful Dee Stone stay with him in the face of certain death?

Why do the C.I.A. want them dead and why are the Nicaraguans so willing to help assassinate them?

How can one little robbery make one fat Englishman so many high powered enemies?

How can one broke unarmed overweight conman on the run threaten the stability of the United States?

What is the secret of the little store in Miami?

When the Government is partners with the mob – there's no hiding place for the Fat Man in America.

From the headquarters of the C.I.A. to the banking halls of Europe, the word is out – Bury the Fat Man.

Paperback price £4.95 net U.K.

YELLOW BRICK PUBLISHERS. 2, Lonsdale Road, Queens Park, London. NW6 6RD.

AUTOBIOGRAPHY

GANGSTERS LADY.

ELLEN CANNON.

The story of ELLEN CANNON'S life tells what it's like being a member of one of Notting Dale's largest families. This Book is packed with incidents. As her man rose through the ranks of villainy and became a major gangland figure, she was introduced into the society of London's top Jollies of the underworld.

She learned to play the game of the gangsters lady in strict accordance with the rules. Whatever knowledge she had of the secrets of gangland she kept to herself. Now for the first time she's telling all.

She pulls no punches and gives a documented account of the violent life with her husband.

She is a remarkable lady.

Paperback price £4.95 net U.K.

YELLOW BRICK PUBLISHERS. 2, Lonsdale Road, Queens Park, London. NW6 6RD.

CARDBOARD CITY.

JOE CANNON.

What turned a happy family man with an infant daughter to drink? When his money ran out, he found refuge among London's homeless beneath the arches of Waterloo Bridge. Living amongst a community of the homeless and the hopeless where society's outcasts sleep in cardboard boxes. This is a harrowing story marked by scenes of violence.

This book tells the story of Tommy Hutton? Who is he?

Paperback price £4.95 net U.K.